Contents

Acknowledgements

I should like to give my heartfelt thanks to my family, who always pull out all the stops to help me when I am writing, when I need to switch off from daily duties and immerse myself in the work. Hannah, thank you for organising the running of the household at crucial moments, such as ensuring Christmas food shopping was done, meals planned, and for keeping the nurturing side of family life strong, as well as just being there at the right time for cups of coffee together and fascinating conversations about creativity. Ian, thank you for understanding my need to rush off and jot something down that I might forget, and as always for asking me difficult questions that are so helpful. Tom, without you the book could not have taken the form it did. Your sensitive photography, which tuned into the subject with such uncanny understanding, has been of central importance, as it was in previous books you took photographs for, namely, *Helping Young Children to Play*, *Learning through Play: Babies, Toddlers and the Foundation Years* and *Developing Learning in Early Childhood*. Thank you to the Vaughan family, for your enthusiasm and help. I also thank my parents, who have, throughout my life, encouraged my creativity. To all of you, thank you for the fascinating discussions about creativity.

Thanks to Elizabeth Bevan Roberts for her quiet, wise backstage support, Anne-Louise de Buriane, Lynne Bartholomew, Jenny Spratt, Maggie Hutchison, Ruth Forbes, Kevin Winningham and my colleagues at London Metropolitan University, to Linda Pound, Penny Holland and Julia Manning-Morton for our important meanderings about children learning to be creative. Special thanks to Tess Robson and the staff, parents and children at Tachbrook Nursery School and to Katrina Foley and the staff, parents and children at Southway Nursery School, Adam, Har, Kim-Anh and Lauren.

A huge thank you to Camilla Curtis, my physiotherapist; without her creative thinking in the use of her expertise, this book, and that before it, could not have been written because the physical constraints would have defeated me.

The author and publishers would like to thank the following for permission to reproduce material in this book:

Page 3, poem reproduced with permission from Peter Dixon; page 17, poem reproduced with permission from Sybil Marshall; page 146, reproduced with permission from Pearson Education.

Every effort has been made to obtain necessary permission with reference to copyright material. The publisher apologise if inadvertently any sources remain unacknowledged and will be glad to make the necessary arrangements at the earliest opportunity.

Dedication

David Lowe retired in July 2003 after ten years as deputy headteacher at Tachbrook Nursery School. His unwavering focus on the children and reflective interactions with them were an inspiration to all his colleagues.

Introduction

Suddenly a subject which has been one of my main areas of interest, together with childhood play, has become a government priority and initiative in education. Creativity is the word of the moment. But for me it has been a word that has resonated for a lifetime. I have always considered creativity to be at the heart of what an educated person needs to be. I thought this even before I left school. I noticed that teachers who brought out and cultivated creativity in the children they taught developed a love of learning in a way that teachers who emphasised conformity and rule of grammar did not. Learning was pedestrian with those procedure-bound teachers. I wrote about the teachers who cultivated creativity, with whom I was fortunate to learn, in a chapter of a book edited by Lesley Abbott and Helen Moyles for the millennium, because I wanted to honour them.

I remember with pleasure how our children would try to fend off bedtime with the cry, 'But I can't stop doing this painting, or making this model, or building this den, or playing this story,' and so on and so forth, 'because … it's creative!'. They knew I would not be able to resist.

Creativity, like play, is a deeply complex concept. It spreads beyond the narrow mono-dimension of what happens in schools and educational settings, and is to be found in the arts, sciences and humanities, across time and space. Creativity is a worldwide issue, which holds in it the essence of what it is to be a fulfilled and fully functioning person. It celebrates the possibilities of the human mind.

Because of the complexity of the subject of creativity, this book is organised to have layers, so that readers can plunge deep or float on the surface, according to interest, need or mood.

The first layer is to be found by simply looking at the photographs, reading the bullet points and the text in the boxes. This will give the key messages and arguments.

The next layer lies beneath the surface, and shows the practical ways in which creativity can be cultivated. The reader can access this by reading Chapters 3–9, inclusive.

The deepest layer shows the philosophical bases, the research and theoretical evidence on which this book rests.

I have held, across the years, recurring themes amongst the multi-faceted layers of fascinating glimpses at the workings of the minds and physical life of young children. These include the uniqueness of each child and, alongside this, their creativity, and the way that play supports and nurtures this, and so much else too. The children who are different demonstrate this uniqueness powerfully, emphasising how we cannot make one size fit all, and how children need to be respected as individuals. I continue to be excited and impressed by the flexibility of children's thinking, the amazing ideas that children have, but also by the reassuring ways in which they show they are part of the human race through the familiar patterns in their thought across the world. I worry, as I have always done, about the deep feelings that children have, and their goodness, their lovingness, their trust, if they are allowed to develop it. The responsibility that we have as adults not to let them down weighs heavy in what frequently seems to be a climate hostile to their needs, and lacking in understanding of what those needs are. Part of this is the neglect, so often found, of the nurturing of their physical embodiment of self which makes them who they are, and enables their self-identity and self-esteem to develop positively. The subtle ways in which children communicate are a challenge to us to become expert, knowledgeable and understanding of their thoughts, feelings, relationships with us, their ideas and very physical lives.

This book is for readers in Further Education colleges, studying for Foundation Degrees and Early Childhood Studies Degrees, as well as for those who have experience of working with young children, wishing to update or renew their knowledge through in-service training. But, as always, I hope that the book does not have a simplistic approach, because we need to understand that working with young children and their families is not a simple thing. Therefore, in this book, as well as writing about creativity simply, I have tried to show the layers which deepen our understanding and enable us to work with ever-greater expertise and sensitivity with young children and their families.

The aim is that, having read the book, those at the beginning of their journey will be in a stronger position to cultivate creativity than they were before reading it. The book also gives glimpses of the layers of understanding and expertise that are there to be learnt about, studied and taken into our practice if we are really to meet children's needs in more than a superficial way. When we study creativity – what it is, how it comes about in the lives of not just children but adults too – we begin to see that we need to keep learning for the sake of the children and their families, as well as for the enriching of ourselves.

Beginning to be creative, being creative and becoming a creator is an enriching aspect of our lives that aids the kind of fulfilment that goes beyond being happy or playful. If we want children to deepen the quality of their lives intellectually, using their minds and feeling comfortable in their bodies and with themselves, emotionally and physically, then we need to cultivate creativity in ourselves too. Otherwise we will offer children rigid, narrow experiences and pedestrian, uninteresting lives.

I hope that this book will encourage readers to continue their own education, to study the arts, sciences and humanities, so that they will have something more to offer the children and families with whom they work. We owe it to the children to be as educated as we can manage in these deep ways. This is not narrow 3R schooling or hoop-jumping academic learning. It is educative learning, which feeds our hearts as well as our minds. On my wall I have a quotation from Maslow, the exact source of which I do not have for it has been there for me to read and remember for so many years. It says:

If you deliberately plan to be less than you are capable of being, then I warn you that you will be deeply unhappy for the rest of your life. You will be evading your possibilities.

We need to make working with young children a thinking profession, a creative profession. The practitioners who work with other people's families must be highly educated, creative learners, well trained to know how children develop and learn. They must be sensitive and able to use their observations to support children's emerging creativity and to cultivate it, so that they, together with their families and carers, use their minds and bodies fully, and in so doing are fulfilled, unique, individual people.

CHAPTER I
CAN ANYONE BE CREATIVE?

We often hear people say, 'I'm not creative'. Perhaps they are not. But that might be because they have never been encouraged to be creative.

Isadora Duncan, a great innovator of dance in the early twentieth century, whose creativity developed a new strand of modern dance based on natural movements such as running, jumping and skipping, wrote in her book:

I wonder how many adults realise that by the so-called education they are giving their children, they are only driving them into the commonplace and depriving them of any chance of doing anything beautiful or original. (Duncan, 1930: 30)

This book shows how parents and practitioners who:

* live with, work with and love children;
* are committed to helping them learn deeply;
* want to do so in ways which are satisfying to the child as a learner;
* want to work with children in ways which encourage them to go on learning

can give children more than pedestrian, uninspiring, commonplace learning experiences, and help them to be, as Isadora suggested, original, innovative and creative learners, with a will to keep learning.

There is much confusion about creativity. We need to dispel such confusion, because it is holding back our work with children and constraining their possibilities to become creative learners.

Dispelling some myths about creativity

The myth that creativity is an innate gift or talent

There is a strong tendency to believe that creativity is a gift with which only some people are born. It seems to run in families. We hear people say, 'They are a very musical family', and it seems that each new generation is as musical as the last. Perhaps the family has developed ways of encouraging the creativity of its children, so that they are, throughout their lives, creative learners. Perhaps more families could be musical, artistic, scientifically and humanistically creative, given more help in knowing how to encourage it.

We need to overcome the myth that creativity is a gift, an innate talent, that you are born either with or without. This book will show that creativity is an important part of every human life. We can cultivate creativity in every baby, toddler and child, and hope that it will continue into adult life. Human brains allow us to:

* move (sitting, crawling, lying down, or walking, running and jumping);
* learn though our senses and movement feedback;
* develop embodiment and a sense of self as separate from but connected to others;
* communicate in words, intonation, pauses, cadence and rhythm, gestures and body language;
* have ideas and thoughts;
* have feelings;
* develop relationships;
* play so that we are innovative, flexible and are not pinned down to one result;
* imitate by reconstructing what others do;
* make mental images (visual, auditory, olfactory, taste, tactile) and imagine;
* remember;
* represent, keeping hold of our experiences and going beyond the here and now;
* become a symbol user by making one thing stand for another;
* be creative, giving an existence to ideas, thoughts, feelings, relationships and physical embodiments.

All of these brain processes contribute to and help in the cultivation of creativity. They are each important in different ways. Creativity emerges out of the co-ordination of these broad-ranging processes.

The myth that only a genius can be creative

In this book we shall explore different kinds and layers of creativity. We shall focus on what it means to be a creative learner. It is very rare for someone to bring unique, completely original creativity to the world, but we can be everyday creators and, in doing that, we shall enrich our lives and our learning.

Original and world-shaking creativity

We shall look at truly **original creativity**, which is rare to find, because it is an act of creativity that is unique in human history. However, because it is so unusual, we shall not make this the main focus of the book. We do need to bear in mind, though, that we may be teaching or have in our group a child who will either be encouraged or constrained by us, but who will one day become a famous creator. This amusing poem by Peter Dixon helps us to think about this!

Calling the Register

Teachers never know what might become of the faces in their classes:

Pens down…
I said 'pens down' Tolstoy,
And that includes you Shakespeare…
And you Brontë.
Right – look this way everyone –
Nelson, I said *this* way.
That's better…
And you can take that grin off your face Groucho –
Nobody thinks you're funny.
Right – this way everyone.
Marconi, did you hear what I said…?
And where do you think you're going Oates?
And you Magellan, just sit yourselves down.
That's better.
Stop waving your arm Hitler!
That's much better, much better.
Gogh… leave your ear alone,
And don't touch that piano Beethoven.
OK everyone –
See, you can be sensible when you want to be,
Even you Da Vinci,
And you Einstein.
Picasso stop doodling –
Art lesson's over,
It's time for the poetry programme.

Who knows how to switch the television on?
No, not you Baird.
Livingstone, you can do it today…
Livingstone?
Livingstone?
Has anyone seen Livingstone?
Sit down Stanley!

Recreating an idea in a different time and place

Another aspect of creativity is that sort of creativity which repeats itself in different parts of the world at different times. There is a great deal of re-inventing the wheel. The Romans invented under-floor central heating, which was re-invented at a later point in history. Creations are regularly lost in a particular culture and then found again later by someone creative, or by a creative group of people who co-operate together.

Specialists who create ideas which are important in their field, who may not become famous, but who contribute in important ways

In science, the humanities and the arts, we find people who are very creative and who help their field or discipline to move forward. Some will become well known and famous within or beyond their area of expertise; some will not, and won't become household names.

Everyday creativity that makes life worth living

The major emphasis of this book is on the everyday creativity which can be part of anyone's life, beginning with babies, toddlers and young children, and parents and practitioners working with them. Everyday creativity is what lifts the experience of children and adults out of being pedestrian and commonplace, and enables them to do things which are original and important. This will give them what the psychologist Maslow (in Storr, 1989: 201) calls the ability to become 'lost in the present' because they are able to live the moment to the full. They become 'totally immersed, fascinated and absorbed in the present'. These important moments free us from other people, so that our authentic voice, our deeper self, can emerge and be strong. This is as true for children as it is for adults.

Everyday creativity brings quality to our lives. It is about creative learning and so values the processes of creativity, the developing of ideas alongside the hatching of them. Expert creators, or world-shattering creators, hatch mega-important creations. Most of us bring to fruition creations which are important for us as individuals, within our families and those we love and are loved by. They are just as important as the world-shattering creations. For those who work with or bring up young children, the more we can learn about how to help creative learning for all, the more we help individuals and how they can contribute to the world as well as finding the fulfilment that creativity brings into their lives. Fulfilment is deeper than happiness or enjoyment. It helps us through the difficult times as well as the easier side of our lives.

The myth that creativity applies to the arts more than to the sciences or humanities

One of the most serious problems in relation to creativity is the widely held myth that creativity is a process in the human brain and culture which applies only to the arts. It is rarely discussed in the context of the sciences or the humanities. Unfortunately this is perpetuated in the English curriculum document, *Curriculum Guidance for the Foundation Stage* (QCA/DFES, 2000), as well as the curriculum documents for Scotland, Wales and Northern Ireland. In other countries, where the early childhood curriculum documents do not emphasise areas of learning, this problem does not exist. For example, in New Zealand (Te Whariki).

Creativity in the sciences

Every time a scientist develops a new theory or invention, he or she has created something. The Victorians were great inventors and the Industrial Revolution produced huge changes, with a wealth of new machinery and contraptions of all kinds both at home and in the workplace.

Theories are abstract things, but nevertheless they are creations.

Creativity in the humanities

The humanities are about geography, history, religious and cultural studies. The study of these areas of knowledge leads us to consider issues of equality, human rights, cultural diversity and the environment. For example, the relationship between trans-global corporations and their impact on the environment (Elkington, 2001).

Creativity in the arts

Some art forms use words and signs, but others do not. We respond emotionally to different art forms and the subjects they engage with. We are influenced in doing this by our own interests, by our family and by cultural impact.

Non-verbal art forms
* Dance;
* music;
* visual arts – two-dimensional;
* visual arts – three-dimensional.

Verbal art forms
* Drama;
* poetry;
* literature;
* songs.

Creativity in other aspects of life
* Sports;
* cookery;
* economics.

The myth that performance and creativity are the same

People often confuse performance and creativity. In fact, they are sometimes the same but often they are quite different.

A **performer** takes what, for example, a writer, poet, dance choreographer or music composer has created and **interprets** it.

A director of a theatre, dance or music group will lead the actors, dancers or musicians into an interpretation of the creator's work. The interpretation is the fascination both for the performers and for the audience.

Shakespeare may have written the play *Romeo and Juliet*, but every interpretation is different. The film directed by Baz Luhrman portrayed the text as gang wars between two powerful families in Los Angeles, and the drugs scene. This not something Shakespeare would have known about but it is a valid and fascinating interpretation which works for modern audiences.

A very difficult thing for playwrights, film writers, composers and choreographers is that, unless their work is performed, their creations cannot live. This is why their area of work is called 'the **performing arts**'. Sometimes the writer may also be the performer, but not necessarily.

The place, space and time are important when a creation is performed. For example, Pavarotti singing what is often now called the 'football song', or the Maori dancers at the Opening Ceremony of the Commonwealth Games in 1990.

A potter went to see a performance of the Greek play *The Bacchae* by Euripides, directed by her friend. Afterwards she said to her friend, 'I feel sorry for you, because once the play's season is finished, you have nothing left; but when I create a pot, it remains, unless someone breaks it'. The play director replied, 'But I have made some new friends, and had new thoughts and feelings, which mean that I will never be the same again; nor will the cast or the audience. It's a good feeling. I know myself better than I did before, and I experienced working together in a group to make something together which we could share with audiences. It is an amazing thing, and part of the fascination is the way that each audience is so different, which makes each performance different. The audience influences the way the cast perform. It's all part of the fascination of performance. I wouldn't have missed it for anything. It doesn't matter that it is here and then gone'.

We have all experienced a marvellous performance, whether it is being at a club where the DJ performs the feat of mixing with great skill to make the transition from one record to the next; hearing an orchestra perform at the Albert Hall; seeing Victoria Wood perform at the Albert Hall; seeing Shobana Jayasingh's Contemporary Indian Dance company; or going to a concert at Wembley to hear the 'Brand New Heavies'. Some performances are moments in our lives which we carry with us forever. They are group experiences and the audience is a crucial part of them, as are the performers who interpret the dance, music, plays etc., that either they or others have created.

Improvisations – performers and creators in the same person

Sometimes the performers and the creators are the same people. This is so in the case of jazz or improvised dance and drama. People may have an idea that they develop spontaneously together, taking turns and tuning into each other's ideas. There may or may not be an audience watching and listening. The emphasis here is much more on participation.

In the 1960s the boundaries between audience, creator and performer were experimented with. However, people in the audience often reported that they felt frightened when plucked out of their seats and included in the play – perhaps put on trial as a suspect for Jack the Ripper.

Another example of a performer being a creator is the modern development of the role of the DJ, who improvises scratch music whilst playing the vinyl records chosen for the purpose. This is a popular form of improvisation in clubs, such as the Matrix Club in Reading.

Mixed media

During the 1960s there was also wider experimentation with mixing dance, music, drama and the visual arts, for example in the work of Ian

Spinks and his company, 'Second Stride'. Until then, opera had been the main example of this kind of mix.

In the last few years, there has been greater development in mixing film, dance, drama, music, the visual arts and the use of installations. The performance might take place in a specific place, which cannot be changed. For example, Merce Cunningham, a pioneer choreographer of modern dance, put on performances by his dance company at the Tate Modern Gallery in the Turbine Hall, which is a vast space. The dances would work only if they were performed there. He used architecture, art, film, dance and music, all together.

The visual arts – two- and three-dimensional

Those artists who create paintings, drawings, sculptures or ceramics, or who work with fine arts and crafts, vary in the degree to which they feel the need for an audience. Their creations can exist without anyone seeing or appreciating them. Most artists, however, want to share their work with an audience. Few would say they do not care about whether or not they have an audience, and it is rare that they would argue that they create their work only for themselves. Most visual artists are delighted if people want to buy their creations, to be patrons of their art and fund them, or to see their creations in public exhibitions and galleries. Perhaps, though, it is from the world of the visual arts that the idea of the lonely artist has arisen.

The myth that creative people are unhappy, unstable, difficult temperamentally and unfulfilled

Being creative is not about retreating from unhappiness (Storr, 1989: 123). When we talk about famous creative people, we tend to conjure up visions of artists starving in attics, with their paintings and sculptures unsold. We hear about the struggles of music composers and dance choreographers to have their work performed. We are told about scientists and inventors whose theories and inventions go unrecognised. It is certainly true that most cultures do not reward creativity with high status or remuneration.

We also hear that someone has an artistic temperament or has creative genius, so is liable to outbursts of temper, sulking or sarcasm. As we shall see later in the book, just before our most creative moments we do become physically restless and uncomfortable with ourselves, but this does not have to take the form of unkind or unacceptable behaviour. Many creative people have found ways of dealing with this part of the creative process positively and constructively. There is a great problem only if others expect creative people to be difficult to live with, and make excuses for them to behave thoughtlessly to others. Then there will be a self-fulfilling prophecy, and creativity will be linked with difficult personalities who are unhappy with themselves.

Young people in the UK are choosing to study, in secondary schools and beyond, subjects which explore and encourage creativity, such as the creative arts. It is interesting to consider why this is so. Storr (1989: 123) believes that 'people who realise their creative potential are constantly bridging the gap between the world of external reality and the inner world of the psyche'. Being creative helps us to experience life as worth living.

It may well be the case that creative people are more tuned into their own feelings, thoughts, relationships and bodies, and so are more sensitive and aware of these aspects of living. It means that they are likely to experience life very fully, and so it is important that they are helped from an early age to be courageous learners, with a sense of adventure, able to take risks, to dare to make mistakes and have a go, try alternatives, to rearrange what they know or try out new ways of working. Creative people often remember their childhood vividly, including the pain, joy, humiliations, guilt, shame, unfairness, love and magical moments.

The document *Birth to Three Matters* (DfES, 2002) places great emphasis on:

A strong child:
* me, myself and I;
* being acknowledged and affirmed;
* developing self-assurance;
* a sense of belonging.

A healthy child:
* emotional well-being;
* growing and developing;
* keeping safe;
* healthy choices.

These two 'aspects', the 'healthy child' and the 'strong child', are crucial to the development of creativity. Without these, babies, toddlers and young children are unlikely to develop the other two 'aspects', which are: to be 'skilful communicators' and 'competent learners'. Children who are helped to be skilful communicators are able to find their voice and to make meaning. Competent learners are able to make connections, be imaginative and creative and to represent their experiences, ideas, feelings and relationships. All of these components are important in becoming a creative person.

Our creativity helps us to see the world in different ways, and to make new connections with what we know and feel. Far from creativity causing us to be sad, lonely, unpleasant and unfulfilled, it helps us instead to be integrated people who find our inner selves and unity with ourselves. Froebel, the pioneer educator (1782–1852), held the view that one of the most important things we do when we educate our children is to help them to see themselves in all their relationships. He meant by this that we need to know and relate to ourselves, others and the universe.

Creativity is rather like play. It anchors us and makes us integrated, whole people. Creativity helps us to get our lives 'together'. This similarity between play and creativity was explored in the companion book to this one, titled: *Learning through Play: Babies, Toddlers and the Foundation Years*. In that book, the emphasis was on the ways in which play contributes to learning. In this book, the emphasis is on how creativity, when cultivated, also contributes in deep and far-reaching ways to our learning. Both creativity and play are processes in the human brain which help us to reach our highest moments of learning and understanding.

The myth that children with disabilities and learning difficulties cannot be creative

One of the most amazing things about being a human is the possibility in the brain of going beyond the here and now. We can escape from the immediate present in a way that is unique to life on Earth. We can move into the future and back into the past in ways which allow us to have abstract, original, new ideas and thoughts. This releases us from the constraints of immediate survival and allows us to plan ahead; to use the past as a powerful resource; to rearrange our ideas; alter; adapt; innovate; be original; and to create ideas unique to us, occasionally unique to our culture and, even more occasionally, unique to humanity.

Some children with complex needs and learning difficulties may not develop the possibility for abstract, flexible thinking. However, this does not rule out any chance of the child engaging in acts of creativity. Until the 1970s it was thought that a proportion of children, measured according to IQ, were incapable of being educated. This was found to be untrue. During the 1990s much progress was made in developing the play of children with complex needs and learning challenges (Nielsen, 1992; Orr, 2003). Play and creativity are closely linked, and it is likely that we will make progress in cultivating creativity for all children in the spirit of diversity and inclusion. Just as the development of play can be encouraged in children with disabilities and learning difficulties by emphasising learning through the senses and movement (Bruce, 1991, 2001, 2002), so a similar approach can be taken in cultivating creativity.

On the other hand, children with emotional and behavioural difficulties are often able to access full and rich free-flowing play by using their senses and becoming symbol users, so that they develop their creativity in similar ways to most other children.

The myth that creativity encourages revolution, chaos and anarchy

Humans are social beings. Relationships with other people are important. There is a tendency to conform and do as others do. It is very difficult to be very different. It is only in recent times that people have become aware of the importance of working to develop principles of the equalities (diversity, inclusion, gender, culture and creed, ethnicity disability, age) and to make them central, so that minority groups of various kinds are not bullied, dominated or overwhelmed by majorities and the advantaged.

Famous creative people have all done something different from the usual. Being creative means innovating and doing something original and different from what has gone before. We have seen that the effect on other people of their creations can be disturbing. However, this does not make them revolutionaries or anarchists aiming to bring about chaos so as to destroy the existing stability and order. They are simply people who make us think anew. They challenge us, and sometimes we find that hard. We react in different ways:

* we might be fascinated, and eager to find out more;
* we might be angry because we have to change how we think and do things;
* we might try to stop them, so that we don't have to change.

In fact, one of the signs of intelligent behaviour is the ability to adapt and change, to be flexible and embrace innovation. That doesn't mean change for the sake of change. It means changing because we have new insight and can live more deeply if we adjust to what some creative person or team of people have brought into existence.

Clearing the way for the cultivation of creativity

In this book, the term 'cultivation' is used in Vygotsky's sense. When discussing good ways of helping young children to become writers, he states that:

❊ children must feel the need to write;
❊ they must have a reason of their own for writing;
❊ it must all happen quite naturally.

Vygotsky says:

Writing should be 'cultivated' rather than 'imposed'.

A child approaches writing as a natural moment in her/his development, and not as training from without …

… the best method is one in which children do not learn to read and write but in which both these skills are found in play situations.
(Vygotsky, 1978: 118)

When we try to impose learning of any kind on children instead of cultivating its development, we are likely to put children off future learning. Young children are eager to please the adults they love and spend time with, and so they try to conform to our demands. Sometimes we do more damage than good because of this.

In this chapter we have cleared away some of the confusion that exists about creativity. We have seen that:

CLEARING THE WAY FOR CREATIVITY

☐ Anyone can be creative
☐ But some people are astoundingly creative
☐ Some creative ideas get lost, and are found again by others at different times in history and in different parts of the world
☐ Performance is a means of sharing a creation with an audience
☐ Creative people can be found in every aspect of our lives, including the arts, sciences, humanities, sports and everyday living
☐ Far from being difficult and unhappy, creative people find their lives are inwardly fulfilling and satisfying
☐ Being creative does not make someone revolutionary and dangerous. It means they have new ideas.
☐ The new ideas people have might be new to them, new in their culture and time of history, or new to the world. Every layer of creativity is an important contribution to human living.

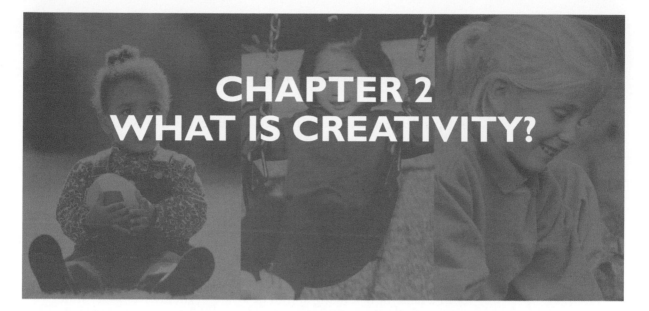

CHAPTER 2
WHAT IS CREATIVITY?

At the beginning of Chapter 1 we saw how Isadora Duncan, the creative dancer in the early 1900s, thought that many children are driven into the 'commonplace' of boring routines and pedestrian activities when they join group settings. This is a serious waste of childhood.

Having dispelled some myths about creativity, in this chapter we are going to establish what creativity is in order to begin to tease out what makes a learning environment that is conducive to the cultivation of creativity. We need to be sure that we know what it is that creative everyday living offers children and the adults who live and work with them. We need to be clear why the cultivation of creativity should have a central place in encouraging the development and learning of children to go beyond the 'commonplace'.

Creativity and the individual

The need for love, companionship and feeling we matter to others

Every child growing up has a need to feel that they are loved and that they matter to at least someone. Companionship that gives love, warmth and affection is part of this. Feeling we belong with others is central to developing well-being. So is being acknowledged and affirmed (DFES, 2002).

This is very different from saying that children should always be socialising and interacting with other people. We all need personal space. Otherwise we cannot develop our self-identity and be self-aware individuals. The original meaning of the word 'individual', according to Abbs (in Storr, 1980: 80) was 'indivisible and collective'. Now it means the exact opposite. 'Individual' in modern usage means being a distinct person, aware of and conscious of our separate self.

Being creative encourages us to know ourselves and gives us independence and a sense of agency. This means that we do not feel under the control of others, and that we can do things ourselves. The *Birth to Three Matters* Framework for England (DfES, 2002) emphasises that a part of being a strong person is feeling self-assured.

The need to know ourselves and to be autonomous individuals

In order to be strong, competent learners, children and adults need both a sense of belonging and to be aware of themselves as separate, creative individuals. The neurologist Antonio Damasio (1999) believes that self-awareness is an important part of the creative process.

Belonging but separate

Children who are encouraged to develop their creativity are helped to develop a point of view of their own, which will not be over-dependent on others. Research shows (Bettelheim, 1977; Storr, 1989: 81; Kitsinger, 1997) that when children do everything as a group, they develop a group identity with shared feelings. This seems to discourage creativity. This is because they are less likely to do something different from the others. Doing something different, new and original is central to creativity. Creativity is part of the process through which children begin to find out they have something unique to 'say', in words or dance, music, or hatching out their theory. They begin to see that, 'Only I can do and say what only I can do!'.

Developing our interests

Having and developing our own interests is an important part of our lives, and is linked with creativity. If we always depend on other people, expect to share all our activities and daily lives with others, and depend on having close relationships with other people as the main source of satisfying lives, then we cannot be fully functioning individuals. We won't have any interests that are our own, so we won't have the possibility to develop, through our creativity, our ideas and points of view. This means we won't be able to bring into existence new ideas, do things in a new way, or make things that are different. We will always follow the crowd. The *Curriculum Guidance for the Foundation Stage* (QCA/DfES, 2000) stresses the importance of identifying and developing the interests of children.

Enjoying and being able to use our personal space creatively

Winnicott (1969: 29) argues that enjoying our own company is a positive thing and a sign of emotional maturity. The journey towards this begins when babies and toddlers enjoy personal space while in the company of people they love and are comfortable with. Because they don't have to worry about things, because they feel safe and secure, they begin to explore their feelings and ideas, to make discoveries and be inventive and innovative. They can become creative. What they do might not be original, world-shaking acts of creation but it is new to them, and so it is an example of what we are going to call 'everyday creativity'.

Some of us continue to enjoy being alone in the company of friends and people who are important to us, taking our personal space and developing our deepest thoughts and creativity in that context. Others like to be alone, having learnt as babies and young children to think well, with creativity and insight, during times of complete personal space.

Winnicott's (1969) theory has helped us to think about the beginnings of creativity, and Vygotsky (1978) is also very useful in this respect. He suggests that the highest forms of thinking begin in a social relationship. Here we see the baby and the adult together, but giving each other personal space in which the baby can discover how to be a creative, thinking, reflective person.

Feeling emotionally safe enough to be creative

In the last chapter we saw how important it was to dispel the myth that creativity requires a state of emotional instability or neurotic personality. Winnicott shows us that the opposite is true. In order to be creative we need to feel sufficiently emotionally safe to go on creative adventures on our own. We have to be apart from others in our minds.

We need companionship and love, and to feel that we are part of things, but we also need to have the personal space to be independent, separate, autonomous, with ideas of our own and to be creative. We belong, yet we need to be separate from others too.

Being a creative person brings a different kind of satisfaction to life. People who depend on the group to tell them how and what to think are not very confident about life. They are anxious about being alone, because they can't think things through or decide what to do on their own. They can't find their own way. Creative people can do this. They are good problem solvers. They like adventures with ideas. They are fascinated by the creative experience of thinking of new ideas.

A creative person's most significant moments are those which give new insight and new discovery, often alone. But daring to think for yourself and to have your own ideas require the courage that comes from being emotionally able to do this. Early positive experiences of being alone, but feeling connected to others, are an important part of this. Vygotsky gives us the cognitive theory why this is so. Winnicott helps us to understand the emotional reasons.

Group creativity

In cultures in which the purpose of painters, sculptors, dancers, musicians, storytellers, writers etc. is to serve the community by giving expression to traditional wisdom, techniques are valued but not the creativity of an individual (Storr, 1989). This book is about both individual and group creativity. We have had a brief look at what is involved in individual creativity; now we will consider some of the important issues surrounding the development of group identity.

We saw in Chapter 1 that groups of people join together and share creative ideas, particularly in relation to scientific projects, drama, music and dance improvisations. This is very different from what Storr (1989) calls 'forced gregariousness', which is not a creative experience. Joanna Glover (2000), writing in her book about children composing music, agrees with Storr about the importance of not forcing gregariousness, and giving children opportunities for what he calls solitude and she calls 'aloneness'.

Aloneness with music is essential for the youngest children and important for most children. Group traditions of performance sometimes dominate organisation for composing. Composing alone can be seen as both a creative need and a learning process. 'It is not until a child has all the control in his or her hands, so to speak, that both aurally and kinaesthetically the feeling of making the music comes fully home. The freedom to take flight in an improvisation, unchecked by anyone else, or to find a musical idea, re-run it, transform, repeat and work over something in your own time, alone, allows a train of thought to develop and find its own shape' (Glover, 2000: 130).

This notion of being creative alone whilst in a community of companions is a recurrent theme in the literature on creativity. Being near people who are sensitive to our need to be alone in a crowd is helpful. Sometimes other children and adults are engaged in the same pursuits, but not always. In early childhood settings where children are encouraged to be creative learners, a first glance round the indoor areas and the garden might suggest that children are all doing different things and are not in a group at all, except when gathered by adults into organised group time for stories and singing together. A deeper look reveals that children are grouping themselves according to their interests. Where there is effective pedagogy, adults are linking the way they work with children through their 'direct and indirect teaching' (QCA/DfES, 2000) into their informed and acted-upon observations of children's learning.

Sybil Marshall (1963: 24), a primary headteacher and a pioneer in the teaching of creativity in the 1960s, identified the attributes of what she sees as a true educator.

A TRUE EDUCATOR:
- ☐ **should know what they are trying to teach;**
- ☐ **should be able to help children learn;**
- ☐ **needs to continue with their own learning and education in order to keep broadening and deepening what they know and understand and can share with children and their families;**
- ☐ **understands that talking and teaching are not necessarily the same thing.**

She recommended (page 120) the detailed study of one child in a group (what we now call regular observation of individual children) so that we see children as a collection of individuals rather than individual children as fractions of a group.

The children in her village school were from 4 to 11 years of age. She gave them a group experience of listening to Beethoven's *Pastoral*; she then took them out to 'enjoy the day', which was similar to the one that inspired Beethoven to write the music. They returned to listen to the music again, whilst taking a mid-morning snack together. This gave a shared experience out of which much creativity emerged. One of the older children, Beverley, who particularly enjoyed writing poems, said one day, after sitting without writing anything for some time, 'I simply can't write an end-of-the-day one, but there's another poem that keeps wanting to come about the symphony all together'.

Symphony

The music is slowing,
It's drawing to an end,
The rhythm is flowing
The weaving tunes still blend.

The oboes were singing,
They made a pretty air:
The violins were stringing,
The double bass was there.

The flutes, bassoons, and piccolos
In harmony agree,
And all the swelling music goes
To make the symphony.

(Beverley, in Marshall, 1963: 211)

The children in this school experienced companionship in writing, but were not expected to produce similar poems. They could develop their own ideas without pressure to conform or create. With the pressure off, they had the time to develop their ideas, incubate them, and could find moments conducive to hatching them, as Beverley did in the group-writing workshop. This is the same whether it is a mathematical idea, scientific hypothesis, dance, poem or musical composition.

This links with what Joanna Glover (2000:131) writes about group compositions in music improvisations. The ability to find some group coherence in improvised music-making can find expression in any human group and any setting. Beyond the immediacy of improvisation, young children composing in groups often compose alone, though side by side.

Creativity brings into existence new ideas, original ways of doing things and new creations of all kinds

Peter Hewitt (Chief Executive of the Arts Council for England) says:

We must keep telling those inclined to prescription, art will never be contained, and creativity never controlled ... It thrives in open spaces where it has room to breathe, where people are free to explore. It is by nature resistant to instruction or targeting. The whole point of creativity, as with all forms of innovation, is that it is impossible to know the outcome in advance. (Hewitt, 2002: 29)

This is as true for creativity in the sciences and the humanities as the arts.

> **In this chapter we have considered, what is creativity? Creativity:**
> ☐ **is an individual response;**
> ☐ **requires autonomy and independence;**
> ☐ **needs personal space;**
> ☐ **is about feeling emotionally safe enough to create;**
> ☐ **can be found in groups, but is not responsive to 'forced gregariousness';**
> ☐ **is about having new ideas and ways of doing things.**

CHAPTER 3
WHAT IS INVOLVED IN CREATIVE LEARNING?

Having an idea – where did it come from?

It is usually impossible to know where a creative idea came from or how it developed into a creation of some kind. This is not a conscious process. Arthur Koestler wrote a pioneering book on creativity in which he argued:

The creative act, in so far as it depends on unconscious resources, presupposes a relaxing of the controls and a regression to modes of ideation which are indifferent to the rules of verbal logic, unperturbed by contradiction, untouched by the dogmas and taboos of so-called common sense. At the decisive stage of discovery the codes of disciplined reasoning are suspended – as they are in the dream, the reverie, the manic flight of thought, when the stream of ideation is free to drift, by its own emotional gravity, as it were, in an apparently 'lawless' fashion. (Koestler, 1964: 178)

This means that creative people:
- [ ] are not conscious of how they came to have an idea;
- [ ] have been able to relax the rules of logic they normally apply;
- [ ] have allowed themselves some 'lawless' and dreamlike thinking;
- [ ] have abandoned common-sense thinking;
- [ ] have allowed their thinking to drift and meander;
- [ ] have then pulled it all together into a disciplined act of creation.

The creative process

John Howkins (2001: 16) has developed a five-fold view of the **creative process**, which he calls RIDER. It is a mix of dreams and analysis.

Review: this means taking stock of things and being curious.

Incubation: creativity needs time and opportunity to form an idea, in a relaxed and unpressured way.

Dreams: drifting about in our thoughts frees us from the usual constraints of our lives.

Excitement: this gives us what Howkins (2001:17) calls the possibilities for making 'intuitive jumps and half-calculated sideways movements'. He says that the trick is not to look before you leap!

Reality checks: we need to check that we are not straying too far in our day-dreaming, drifting and meandering thoughts. Otherwise none of the creative thinking can take shape and form.

Harris takes the view that :

Possible or imaginable instances of magic become more widespread as children's grasp of the constraints on what is possible becomes firmer and more wide-ranging. (Harris, 2000: 166)

The creation

This seems to involve two things at once. People often report that they felt a bit like Archimedes did in his bath, or like Beverley, the ten-year-old introduced in Chapter 2 who wrote the poem to the music of Beethoven's *Pastoral*. They feel a sense of heightened awareness, full of energy and life. They are able to hold their focus very fully and very deeply. But at the same time they also feel very dreamy and their thoughts can flow in a surge of clear thinking.

It is the combination of the two and the ability of the creator to pull the two together, which takes a huge amount of energy, that allow the creation to come to fruition. People often become rather uncomfortable and tense just before the surge. Perhaps this is why creative people are seen as tense and difficult to be with. If we try to talk and interact with them just at that time, they will try to block us out, because otherwise they will quite literally lose the moment.

Jung thought that creativity involved a release of what he called 'energy-tension'. Howkins (2001: 5) says, 'He was scathing about his contemporaries' inclination to link creativity and neurosis'. He thought neurosis was an obstacle to creation.

The moment of creation has often been likened to giving birth to a baby. Because of the energy and effort of forming a creative idea which actually shapes into a creation, we tend to be very emotionally attached to what we create.

Sometimes children show no attachment to a painting or model they have made, and show no interest in whether it is put on the wall as a display nor any inclination to take it home with them. At other times they do. Adults working with young children need to understand the difference between finger painting as a creative process, when ideas are probably incubating, and an act of creation. When it is a creation, the child will be likely to show interest, seeing what they have made as a product.

When working with young children, it is probably most important to put a great emphasis on giving children plenty of time and space, with people sensitive to their ideas. It is therefore helpful to examine what is involved in incubation in a little more detail.

Graham Wallas (in Storr, 1989: 25) thought that there is a period of **incubation** in the development of a creative idea. He suggested that this has three stages:

1. preparation;
2. simmering;
3. illumination.

After the period of incubation, a creation might be hatched out. This might be an idea or something tangible, such as a painting, drawing, sculpture, dance, song, poem, story, scientific theory, mathematical formula, social policy, recipe for a food dish, plan for a treat for a relative. Because of the huge effort and energy needed for a creative idea to take form and become a creation, most creative processes do not end with a product. We talk about the best-laid plans, which drift and meander but don't quite take form.

Children who are experiencing trauma, who are unsettled, have a low sense of well being or are put under pressure to conform to adult-led tasks, are unlikely to be able to summon up the energy needed to think creatively and shape these thoughts into creations. This is why it is important that children are given their **right to play** (Hyder, 2004). Play is largely about creating the conditions which are conducive for creativity to develop in both process and product. Whilst they play, children prepare, simmer and illuminate ideas, without pinning them down into creations. Unless the processes of creativity are strong, the creations will not be strong. Play supports the possibility for creative ideas and thoughts to develop. The processes of representation support children's creations.

<u>Photo 1: Helping with setting up</u>

Preparing

Creative babies, toddlers and young children will develop an interest in something and try to find out more about it. They depend on adults to create environments in which they will have enough freedom of choice to do this. They need interesting materials to explore and experiences which capture their interest. They also need adults who will help them by being informed, sensitive observers, who can tune into what it is that they are paying attention to, and who will help them to find out more.

Simmering

Rudolf Steiner (1975) believed that the period of forgetting is as important as the period of remembering. We often say we will sleep on an idea. Gopnik *et al.* (1999) say that we use what we know to make connections with what we don't know, and we need other people to help us in doing this.

In order to be creative, we need personal space and time away from forced gregariousness, to mull things over and subconsciously reflect on what has interested us. We might not even be aware that we were interested in an idea or thing.

Babies and young children depend on adults to create time both to develop interests and to let them simmer and incubate.

Illumination

This involves having an insight into how to take an idea that has been forming into creation. This is sometimes described as having insight, or as the 'a-ha!' experience. One of the most famous examples of this is the story of Archimedes in his bath. He had been gathering thoughts about volume, without really realising it, for some time. These thoughts were simmering in his head, and then, whilst having his bath, he had a moment of insight. The idea was then able to hatch out into what is now known as:

Archimedes Law

When an object is submerged in a fluid, the upward force which this creates on the object is equal to the weight of the fluid which the object has displaced.

Corollary:

If this force is greater than the weight of the object itself, then the object will float. If it is less than the weight of the object, then it sinks.

Hatching

John Howkins (2001: 127) says there are 'commencement' incidents which start an idea going. We don't usually have any awareness that this is happening to us. This occurs during the period of preparation in the incubation process in creating an idea that comes to fruition. Of course, not all creative ideas become creations. They may stay in our heads and lead to other ideas. Some creative ideas might lead us into other creative thoughts. Others emerge from deep inside us and become externalised into creations.

There is the famous example of the creative scientist who went for a walk in the countryside and saw some teasels growing on the riverbank. He thought no more about it. Somehow this memory became used in hatching out the creation of Velcro™, which on one side has teasel-like hooks and on the other side is like animal fur, easy for the hooks to attach themselves to. It has transformed the way we join material together, just as buttons and zips did when they were first invented as improvements on tying with ribbon or lacing.

The gap between the commencement incident during the period of incubation and the hatching out of a creation varies. It could be hours and days, or it could be weeks and years. When we offer children experiences they find interesting, we never know where it might lead, later coming to fruition as a creation.

In his book, *Mind Storms*, Seymour Papert (1980), who developed ideas important in helping people to use computers, especially children, remembers back to his childhood. From an early age he loved cogs. His parents noticed this interest in cogs and encouraged it. When he later created the 'Turtle' computer, which moved about when instructed by children, he made the cover transparent so that they could see the cogs he loved so much inside it.

We can see the creative process leading to a creation here. Papert had plenty of opportunity to gather experiences and ideas abut cogs, encouraged by his parents to do so as a very young child. The idea of using cogs and how they move together became intertwined with his work as an adult and was used in developing machinery. He had all the time needed for this to come together in a powerful mixture and simmer.

His thoughts did come together and connect, so that he gained insight and was able to go the next step and develop his now-formed idea and hatch it out into an early form of computer, suitable for use by children and beginners.

We shall see more examples, from the arts, sciences and humanities, in later chapters.

There is often a heightened awareness as we hatch out an idea. It is a feeling of intensity, very focused and alert. It is a good feeling, although it is often followed by exhaustion and the need to relax. The hatching process must not be interrupted or it will vanish. When moments like this are interrupted, it leaves the person feeling that something has been snatched away, and it is very dispiriting. There is a feeling of loss. After all, as Winnicott (1971: 79) says, creativity 'belongs to being alive'.

The role of the adult in cultivating creativity

Adults play a critical part in whether or not children become creative people. Unless they work sensitively with children and their families, the emergent possibilities for creativity that are in every child do not develop or can be quickly extinguished.

Adults who tune in to what interests the child and who are informed participant observers are able to appreciate and value the beginnings of creativity in children without invading the child's creative idea or taking it over. They support children as they develop their autonomy and value them as individuals. At the same time, they make sure the children feel a sense of belonging.

It is helpful to look at some practical examples of adults working with children, to see what this looks like in reality.

Being there for children – adults as anchors, who make children feel secure enough to let their creative ideas begin to flow

Often, when children arrive in the morning, they need to be near or with an adult they trust and know, with whom they have developed a warm and affectionate relationship. Sensitive companionship, as we saw in earlier sections, cultivates creativity.

Adults can arrange to be an anchor, to sit in one area and 'be there' for children in the spirit of companionship. In the photograph (2), the adult is doing just that. The little girl, who appreciates being with her, shows this in the way that she offers her some pretend food to eat. Although this is a very everyday moment of creativity, it shows that she is sufficiently relaxed to let her ideas flow and make some pretend food. This adult is exceptionally good at working with children in this way. She has the gift of opening children up to learning and having ideas. She sets children on their way to developing their creative ideas further.

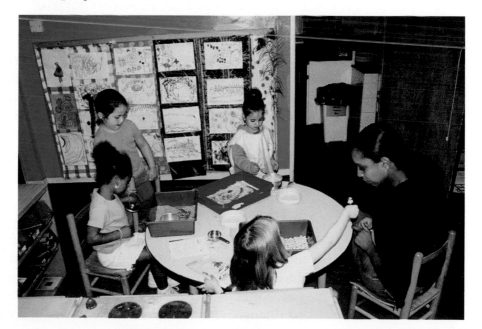

Photo 2

Being near – adults having eyes at the back of their heads, observing and aware, but respecting the children's personal space and joining in only when needed

In the photographs (3, 4) the children are creating ideas around the large hollow wooden blocks. They are trying out sequences. They are very sensitive to each other as they move, and seem to have an idea of how to be responsible for their own safety as they do so.

Photo 3   Photo 4

They climb to the top and then leap off with their own individual style. This is a game that is as old as the history of humanity. It is the sort of thing that makes adults in group care situations indoors feel a bit edgy. However, the adult is nearby, sensitive to the children and their needs, and the children, although exuberant and very lively, are well organised. They take turns, wait for each other to jump, keep an eye to make sure that the blocks are carefully arranged. Interestingly, this creative idea does not develop. They leave after about five minutes.

On another day, there was an imaginary swimming pool, with children jumping into the deep end and other children pretending to be lifeguards. Somehow today the mood and chemistry weren't right and the children abandoned the play. This often happens with a creative idea. For every creative idea, many fall by the wayside. Only a few ideas get through.

Adults guiding the children in order that a creative idea can break through and continue

We frequently find that children become frustrated, get stuck, are about to give up because they hit a problem as they play. We need to remember that, in many respects, free-flow play and developing creative ideas are the same. Neither can be pinned down. Both are about children using their experience to learn more. In free-flow play a creative idea is developed but is in a state of flow. Sometimes these ideas are pinned down and become acts of creation, either then or later. However, this is not always the case.

Returning to some of the significant aspects relating to the development of creativity discussed earlier in the chapter, we can see that there is a delicate balance here between helping the child, and making the child feel a sense of agency and seeing themselves as a separate and independent individual.

Toddlers can be very rejecting of help because they want to be independent, but they can't manage to do what they want to do. This is where adults need to be particularly understanding and sensitive to the child's feelings. By holding a piece of wood still or cutting a tough piece of string, but letting the child participate, constantly checking that this is what the child has in mind, the adult can support a child through a tricky moment in the creative process. Then the moment is not lost, the child has a positive experience and learns that with perseverance an idea can be developed.

In the photographs (5, 6), the two girls are using the hollow wooden blocks but are having difficulty getting the planks to straddle the two sides. They need two planks to cover the distance, but they don't know how to prop them up, or perhaps they don't realise how to prop them up. The adult sees the problem out of the corner of her eye and joins the play. She brings the conversation round to the identification of the problem. As a consequence of the adult doing this, one of the children suggests propping the planks up with a cylinder from the wooden unit block set from the shelf behind. With the problem solved, the children are able to develop their free-flow play which contains in it their creative ideas.

Helping children to know how to use materials

Every material is different and has its own characteristics. We can't expect children to know about paint or clay or dance, and what is involved in engaging with these areas, unless we help them.

<u>Photo 5</u>

<u>Photo 6</u>

In the next photographs, we can see children being supported by adults as they learn about these areas, which are just three examples of the kind of help children need if their creativity is to be cultivated.

⁂ **Clay**: The children have been helping to build a wall in the outside area. This is reflected in the way the clay is provided in that area. By showing an interest and watching what the children are doing, talking to them and listening carefully to the children's ideas, the adult can give the appropriate support to each child (photograph 7). One is interested in cutting the clay but the problem is, how do you cut a rolling ball? The other little girl is making small lumps of clay and putting them on the brick in a row. She is very interested in the other girl's ball and the lumps of clay seem to be getting more and more spherical. Children pick up on and take forward ideas which attract them. We say that imitation is a great form of flattery. Children in group settings learn as much from each other as they do from the adults. Here, the idea of spheres is being incorporated into the creative idea of making a row of small pieces of clay on top of the block.

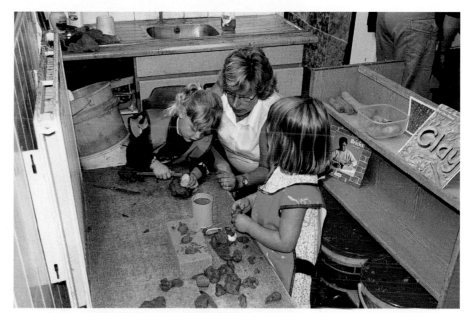

Photo 7

※ **Paint:** The children have made, with the help of the adult, the paint mixture they need for finger painting. They want to keep changing the colours, and decide they would like to add yellow. Because they have paint on their hands, the adult offers to sprinkle some yellow paint in order to help them. There is plenty of discussion about what is needed (photographs 8, 9). It is important to remember that a discussion is a two-way thing. It is not the adult instructing and asking questions that the child is expected to answer as a kind of test. A discussion is when people genuinely interact with each other to make a dialogue together. Doing this helps children to become more aware of their creative ideas, so that they are more likely to turn them into creations. However, finger painting is not about making lasting creations. It is all process. It is about getting to know how paint behaves, and making shapes, patterns and images which are fleeting. It gives children opportunities to gather ideas for future use. This is a huge part of creativity.

Photo 8

Photo 9

Gathering ideas – incubating ideas – hatching ideas

Every time a creative idea is hatched, we need to remember that it rests on an edifice of ideas gathered, built on, rearranged and altered, through a period of incubation. Not all ideas will develop to the point of becoming creations. Creativity is hugely about process, and only sometimes carries through into a product.

In the photographs showing the clay and finger painting the children are gathering and incubating creative ideas. It is not one of those moments when the ideas are turned into lasting creations.

* **Dancing**: Just as the children needed support and help with the clay and the finger painting, so they need help with dancing. They can make a start, by selecting their dancing clothes. Wearing dressing-up clothes often leads into dance or role-play. It helps us all to switch into the mood required for these areas of learning (photographs 10–13). At the moment there is a ballet craze in the setting, and staff have supported this interest by introducing appropriate clothes, music pictures and books. They also provide dance clothes and books about dance in a range of cultures. Once they are in their costumes, the girls want some ballet music to be played. The adult discusses with them what music they would like and, as soon as it begins, they move into attempts at arabesques, toe pointing and second position arm movements. This is creative in the sense that, although they are using ideas they have gathered about dance, they are putting them together in their own way. As so often happens, they are watched with interest by another child, in this case the child on the rocking horse, who may or may not have seen ballet. Observing what other children do is a major way in which children gather ideas which they later use creatively.

Photo 10

Photo 11

Photo 12

Photo 13

The child as a separate individual needing personal space and also feeling connected to others through a sense of belonging

Some people love to be alone in a crowd. The little boy in the photographs (14–19) is very focused. He clearly has an idea in his mind and he does not need the support of others. He is content to work on his creative idea alone and without company. However, he is able to do this because he is settled and at ease in the group setting. Unsettled children cannot develop their creativity. These are the children who worry us because they flit restlessly. Exploring different materials and moving from one to the other when you have an idea in mind which you carry with you is not flitting (Athey, 1990). This has a focus which is missing from flitters.

Photo 14

Photo 15

Photo 16

Photo 17

Photo 18

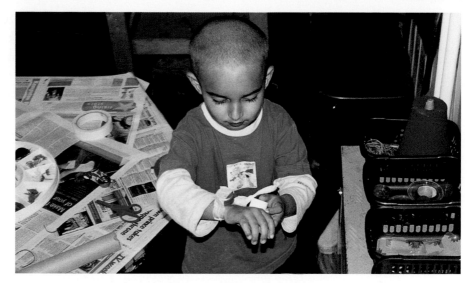

Photo 19

Adults who are good observers of children can see the difference between a focused child developing a creative idea and needing to meander amongst materials and try things out in the service of a thought, gathering form, incubating and simmering, and a child who surges about without stopping to look at all.

The boy has a rotation schema. This means that he likes to wrap things round objects. A schema is a repeatable pattern in the way he does things, which can be generalised to all sorts of situations. He decides to stay at the workshop area, and selects a hollow cardboard cylinder and coloured sticky tape to wrap round it. He then wraps the blue sticky tape around his wrist. He is not flitting, but rather he is elaborating his creative idea by using it again on his wrist. However, this is not matching what he had in mind. He realises this only when he tries it. After a bit of seeking and searching in the boxes on the shelves, which might look to an insensitive observer like flitting, he finds a plastic ring. He puts this on the back of his hand and manages to wrap the blue sticky tape over it. He unpeels it. He meanders about in the boxes again, and then finds a golden plastic bottle top. He unwraps some white tape, which is wider than the blue sticky tape. Once again, he wraps the tape round his wrist and over the bottle top. It seems that he is left-handed. He looks at the tape thoughtfully. He unpeels it and repeats the process, using more white sticky tape and a different bottle top. He leaves it on this time. He has made a watch for himself. His creative idea has come to fruition and he has made a creation – a watch. He does not show this to anyone, but the observant adult asks him a bit later, when he has left the area, 'What's the time?'. He looks surprised. She points to his watch. 'I wondered if that was a watch, but perhaps I am wrong'. He smiles.

It is important to respect the child's creation. Guessing what children have made or drawn or painted can lack sensitivity on the part of the adult. In this case, the adult wanted to show she valued his creation and had noticed it being made. She gave him the opportunity to say it was not a watch. He was pleased that she thought his creation mattered.

In this chapter we have seen how important it is not to give children commonplace experiences. Ellen Langer believes that we need to develop 'mindfulness' in children. She argues that 'Learning the basics in a rote, unthinking manner almost ensures mediocrity'. She gives a powerful example:

At tennis camp I was taught exactly how to hold my racket and toss the ball when serving. We were all taught the same way. When I later watched the U.S. Open, I noticed that none of the top players served the way I was taught, and, more important, each of them served slightly differently ... Even if we are fortunate enough to be shown how to do something by a true expert, mindless practice keeps the activity from becoming our own ... If we learn the basics but do not over-learn them, we can vary them as we change or as the situation changes. (Langer, 1997: 14)

Varying what we know is at the heart of creativity. We need to help our children to dare to be creative, like the little boy making the wristwatch, or the girls varying what they knew of ballet to make their own dances. Varying what we know means daring to be different. That is also at the heart of creativity. If we focus on the basics and teach them in a 'one size fits all' method, we constrain children's possibilities to become creative. We have seen that this will lead to half-lived lives, which are not inwardly satisfying. Instead, we want children to have the energy, focus, diverse ideas, flexible flowing thoughts and deep satisfaction in their learning that bring them alive in the fullest sense of living. Creative learning means living to the full.

In this chapter, we have looked at:
- [ ] where creative ideas come from;
- [ ] how adults can cultivate creativity;
- [ ] adults as anchors;
- [ ] adults who are near and 'on hand' to help;
- [ ] adults knowing when to guide and give direct help;
- [ ] adults helping children to gather ideas, incubate and hatch them.

CHAPTER 4
CREATING AN ENVIRONMENT
THAT CULTIVATES CREATIVITY

We know that people who love and help children to develop and learn are the most important thing in their lives. If children are to develop their creativity, they certainly need adults who cultivate this side of their learning. We need to remember that part of the adult's role is to create both an atmosphere and an environment that cultivate creativity.

In this chapter, we shall explore how we can set up the indoor area with creativity in mind. The environment plays a central part in cultivating creativity. But if organised wrongly, it can constrain or even extinguish it.

We can do so much to encourage creativity in children and in ourselves if we think carefully:

* about the materials we offer as experiences;
* about the way we offer the material provision.

We know that the physical, direct experiences children have are fundamental to their learning about a sense of self through embodiment and connectedness to others; and we also know that these are the bases of symbolic behaviour and creativity of all kinds.

The way that we help children to interact with the material and experiences we provide will have a great impact on whether or not they develop into creative people.

Sensitive interaction on the part of adults, together with a carefully thought-through provision of the physical environment, is the key to the cultivation of creativity.

Before the children arrive

Let's look at the way staff in one setting lay out some of the provision ready for the children to arrive first thing. There are two rooms, a coat area, entrance hall and corridor to make ready for the arrival of the children and their parents. Parents are welcome to stay as long as they like and settle their children in. Some of the children will stay all day and some will attend for either the morning or the afternoon.

The material, physical environment needs children in it to make it come alive, and so there is always a feeling of uncanny quietness and anticipation of things about to happen when setting up the learning environment. It's a bit like a stage set before a rehearsal or a dance studio before the dancers arrive. Nevertheless, it is useful for us as practitioners to take a good look at how carefully we are thinking through our provision for children. They will not get much out of their time in a group setting if this is not an intrinsic part of the way the staff work together.

Creative entrance areas

The first thing the children will see will be the entrance hall. This is where children are greeted and signed in each day by a member of staff. It is an important part of the learning area, because this is a cramped building and every bit of space is creatively put to use by the staff and children. It is full of nooks and crannies, which are very appealing to children. Later in the day, a volcano will erupt here, and a very imaginative scene will emerge, initiated by the children.

Photo 20

Next door there is a cloakroom for coats. There is a fish tank full of fish on a low cupboard, before which children often like to stand and watch, and there are books which cultivate imaginative scenes. These have emerged out of previous play scenarios and serve as reminders to children of past play episodes that went well. Sometimes the books become prompts which re-activate a play idea. Sometimes children simply enjoy looking at the books (photograph 20).

Creative use of rooms

The children arrive each day knowing that there will be interesting things on offer and knowing that there will be things specially for them as individuals. Because observation is at the heart of the teaching, and informs it, the staff use their observations of children at play to help them plan both for the group and for individual children's learning (Bartholomew and Bruce, 1993; Hutchin, 2003).

Creativity is an interesting area to plan for. This is because we don't know in advance how a child might show their creativity. The important things are:

❋ to get the indoor and outdoor environments organised so that they support the cultivation of creativity;

❋ that adults understand and are informed about how to help creativity to develop.

The children can go through either of two doors to enter the two rooms, which have a connecting door between them. Wherever they go, everything is carefully laid out and presented. The environment sends signals to the children about how they might use it. The children have free access to the outdoor areas throughout and at group time, when the weather allows, they may go to the garden for their story, poetry, singing and dancing. Each child has a key adult with whom they go for group times, but they are free to use the whole of the indoor and outdoor areas throughout the rest of the session. This is what might be called a 'yes' environment. It beckons to be used.

PRESENTATION OF MATERIALS
- ☐ Displayed at child height
- ☐ Clear categories and sorted carefully
- ☐ A designated area of the room where the materials can be used nearby
- ☐ Labels with pictures and words

Wooden unit blocks

For example, the wooden unit blocks are in wheeled storage containers. They can be taken into different areas when the children need them to add to their play but, on the whole, they remain in an area where they are set out on storage shelves (book shelves). The drawings of the unit blocks, with labels on them, show the children what is there.

On this particular day, staff have planned to offer the wooden marble maze alongside the wooden blocks, because they are following up the interests of one particular child. It will be interesting to see if the child takes up the offer. When we talk about teaching children, we need to bear in mind that children cannot be forced to learn something. They have to want to learn it, or it just won't happen. They will learn to perform tricks to please adults, but that is not the kind of deep and real learning that is the subject of this book.

In one room there is the set of wooden unit blocks. These all relate to each other mathematically. In this book, unit blocks are recommended for this reason: if we are going to go to the expense of a set of wooden blocks, we want to buy a set which offers the maximum possibilities.

whole unit							
$\frac{1}{2}$				half unit			
$\frac{1}{4}$		$\frac{1}{4}$		$\frac{1}{4}$		$\frac{1}{4}$	
$\frac{1}{8}$	$\frac{1}{8}$	$\frac{1}{8}$	$\frac{1}{8}$	$\frac{1}{8}$	$\frac{1}{8}$	$\frac{1}{8}$	$\frac{1}{8}$

Mathematical relationships between Community Playthings™ Unit Blocks

The wooden unit blocks are the modern form of Froebel's Gifts. Plastic blocks are rarely satisfactory because they are so difficult to balance. They are too flimsy and light, and easy to knock over. The wooden blocks should be made from wood grown in sustainable forests. A set of wooden blocks, preferably unpainted so that the grain of the wood can be experienced, is probably one of the most important materials we offer children in group settings.

Wooden unit blocks in home and group settings

Grandparents will sometimes save up to buy wooden unit blocks for their grandchildren as a major gift to last a whole childhood. Adults take great pleasure in them too, because they are so beautiful to hold and use. A set of wooden unit blocks can lead to some marvellous family times, full of creativity on the part of both the adults and children taking part.

Sets of wooden unit blocks are sometimes on loan from toy libraries and local authorities, Early Years Partnerships, voluntary organizations and childminding networks, for accredited childminders to use in their homes.

Hollow wooden blocks

Outdoors, children at Tachbrook are offered the large hollow blocks. In this nursery school, where space is at such a premium, it makes sense to have this provision outside, because this is the only place where there is the space to make large constructions. Some settings also use mini hollow blocks.

Construction sets

In the other room, there is one large construction kit. It is very important to differentiate between construction kits and wooden block play:

* **wooden blocks** are **free-standing**, and **balancing** them is an important part of their use;
* **construction kits** are made up of **pieces that connect together** in various ways, with slots, screws, nuts and bolts, and interweaving spikes.

It is best to choose only two types of construction set, one larger scale than the other. Then these can be added to, so that children have sufficient material to use. There is nothing more frustrating than not having enough blocks or pieces of the construction kit when you have an idea you want to carry out. Getting the creative idea out of your head and into the blocks or construction kit so that it becomes an act of creation depends on having enough material to do that.

CREATIVE BLOCK PLAY AND CONSTRUCTION PLAY DEPEND ON:
☐ adults who set up the materials so that they are conducive to creative ideas and acts;
☐ having the materials;
☐ giving children freedom of choice and time to use the materials;
☐ giving children a broad, rich range of experiences so that they are able to develop plentiful ideas to use creatively.

Block and construction materials are expensive, and will need to be carefully budgeted for. Group settings will need to include this kind of planning in their development plans. Perhaps a few blocks or construction pieces can be bought each year, and an ample set of pieces will gradually develop over the years.

As photographs 21 and 22 show, there is an area indoors set up for large construction experience but children can also take smaller construction pieces from a shelf. They may also use both types of pieces outside.

Photo 21

Photo 22

Children often prefer to construct when sitting on the floor, but it is also good to offer opportunities for working on a table.

It is worth thinking about which materials will be costly and which won't, and planning with both in mind. Cardboard boxes, for example, cost nothing. Arranging a supply (e.g. collecting boxes from a supermarket on a certain day regularly) can bring good community links, with everyone thinking about how to help the children develop their creativity. Balancing tins and boxes of food gives a building experience for children too. This will not harm the food, which can be replaced in the cupboard later.

In both home and group care settings, with low or high budgets, we can provide opportunities for children to build and construct. However, ideally we will manage to provide some kind of wooden unit blocks and one carefully chosen construction set so that children can have deep and life-lasting experiences which will impact on their ability to be creative in this area.

Adults who become engineers, architects, theatre set designers and dramatists (creative writers in theatre) or novelists and story-writers often say how much they enjoyed playing with blocks and construction kits as children.

Famous examples would be:
* architect – Frank Lloyd Wright (whose mother was a Froebel-trained kindergarten teacher and provided him with wooden unit blocks at home);
* writer – E.E. Nesbitt, who wrote stories for children;
* writer – H.G. Wells, who wrote stories and science fiction;
* writer and poet – Robert Louis Stevenson, of *A Child's Garden of Verses*.

The woodwork area

Woodwork, like block play and construction, is another form of material provision that offers experiences which are invaluable to children in all aspects of their development and learning, particularly their creativity.

In setting up all areas of the learning environment, whether indoors or outdoors, it is of paramount importance that children are safe. Risk assessments need to be made in order to make sure that children can experience full learning opportunities. Safety awareness should open up, and not close down, learning opportunities. Part of ensuring safe learning environments is for staff or those at home to think through what is necessary for this. The other part is to educate the children into thinking about their own safety and that of their friends as an important part of their learning.

The woodwork area, like every other area of provision, needs to be set up with great care. It is more important here than in other areas, however, to be able to tell at a glance which tools are not in their designated place. Children should return them here when they have finished using them.

If the area becomes very popular (there are usually some days more than others when this is so), a waiting list can be useful. There are examples of notices which can be used in this way in the photograph (23). Most of the time, when equipment is available every day, there is not much need to restrict the number of children. However, at a woodwork bench, staff clearly need to be able to work effectively with children, and children must not be crowded in case they accidentally hit a neighbour with a hammer or saw a person rather than the wood.

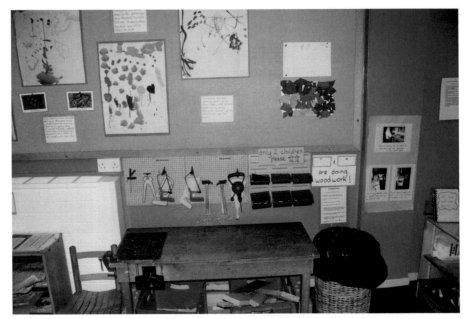

Photo 23

There are various styles of setting up woodwork areas. In this book several different woodwork benches are shown (others can be seen in Bruce, 2004). The important thing is that staff think carefully about how best to offer woodwork experiences to children. Both in the traditional Scottish approach, seen in other parts of this book, and in the presentation here, the same principles are used:

THE WOODWORK AREA

- [ ] everything has a place;
- [ ] little is more – which means that there are one or two hammers and saws, and one of other tools;
- [ ] there is a vice to hold the wood still with safety;
- [ ] the tools are easy for children to use, and selected with that in mind;
- [ ] numbers are limited, with a waiting list system to ensure equality of opportunity and to make sure less assertive children have their turn;
- [ ] the area is available for the whole session because it is located where an adult is always nearby;
- [ ] there is a plentiful supply of easy-to-saw-and-nail wood, that is not too liable to splinter;
- [ ] there are photographs on the wall of children using the area;
- [ ] there is an expectation that children will use the area responsibly, and children are fully confident because they understand the clear boundaries that have been established to keep them safe;
- [ ] there is discussion of safety issues as well as discussion of creative ideas coming to fruition as wooden creations between adults and children.

Workshop area

The workshop area is usually placed near to the woodwork area, and this is so here. There is a table with basic equipment on it, such as glue, masking tape, Sellotape™, pencils for labelling or decorating, left- and right-handed scissors (photograph 24).

Photo 24

<u>Photo 25</u>

On shelves next to the table are enticing boxes with materials that can be used for collage or model making (photograph 25). Above this there are constructions made by the children, with labels explaining what they are about. Adults have scribed what the children have told them, or children have made their own marks. This gives status to the creative ideas which have become creations in the form of models.

There is less of an issue about numbers of children using the workshop area at any one time, because safety is not such a concern. Children can sit on chairs if they wish or they can stand at the table. They often choose the latter, so that they can potter about as they develop an idea. We know from research on the brain that it is difficult to think whilst sitting still (Goddard-Blyth, 2000). Children who are free to move are free to think fully. They may sit down if they want to be at a particular angle or in order to co-ordinate a movement when working to create something.

The same principles are used in every area of provision, indoors and outdoors, but every area has its particular contribution and character. Many parents and childminders now have areas that are workshops on a miniature scale. There might be a drawer in a unit at child height in the kitchen, with masking tape, pot of glue, scissors etc. in it, and a box of straws, buttons, scraps of material, sticks, stones etc. which the children can use while sitting at the kitchen table to create models. The workshop area also has these principles which guide its use and presentation:

WORKSHOP AREA

☐ there is a table or working surface on which children can create things;

☐ an adult is available to support the child's creative idea, and help the child transform the idea in their head into a creation. (This is very different from the adult helping the child to make something that is an idea in the adult's head come to fruition, using the child as a vehicle for the adult's creative idea!);

☐ children can see what is on offer, with clear presentation of materials;

☐ the surfaces are easy to clean and children are not nagged about making a mess;

☐ there is plenty of time for creative ideas to be mulled over, and no pressure to turn these into creations. The processes of creativity are valued;

☐ when children do turn a creative idea (process) into a creation (product), and want to keep it, or take it home later, this is valued and appreciated, and placed in an area with a label.

Painting

There are times when children want to paint and want to find the colours and paper available and ready to use. Their creative idea might be constrained by having to mix colours. This would slow down their flow of thoughts (photographs 26, 27).

There are other times when they want to mix their own colours and to experiment. There should therefore always be the opportunity to do this. There will usually be children in a group who have an idea which they have been incubating and that is ready to come to fruition. Then they may have definite ideas about what colours they need, and so will

Photo 26

Photo 27

express their idea more as they want it if they can mix the colours themselves.

In the same way, when children first begin to try to set down on paper their story-writing ideas, they often need an adult to scribe for them. Otherwise they get bogged down in the mechanics of writing, while the ideas that they are trying to express evaporate.

We are inclined seriously to underestimate the creativity of children. This is probably because we seriously neglect our own creativity. Either it was never developed in us and so we don't know what it is, or we have let it go, by allowing our lives to become dominated by the 'commonplace' events, as Isadora Duncan calls them, of daily living and working. This is a terrible waste of brainpower. The legally enshrined document in England, *Curriculum Guidance for the Foundation Stage* (QCA/DfES, 2000) describes teaching as 'helping children to learn'. This means helping children to use their brains to the full.

Materials to explore

One of the things adults often recall from their childhood play is the memory of making mud pies in the garden. In Tachbrook there is a digging-in-the mud patch outside, but indoors the experience is offered in a different form. Some children don't like to feel they are getting dirty and they appreciate making mixtures with 'clean' materials (photograph 28).

<u>Photo 28</u>

There are definite points of view about using food for play, and not all settings do so. The argument for using flour to make dough, or lentils and pasta for mixtures, is that they last a long time, and only food that is beyond its sell-by date is used and so could not be used for food preparation.

Puzzles and games and looking at detail

This area is very clearly set out, in an attractive area near the entrance to the room. This is very helpful for children who appreciate a cosy corner, where they can quietly settle at something they feel secure in doing. Games are very comforting when they are familiar and well known. This is also a good spot for an adult to sit first thing in the morning, so that children who are a bit more timid about coming to the group will feel welcomed and can find something to do that is comfortable, with an adult to support them (photograph 29).

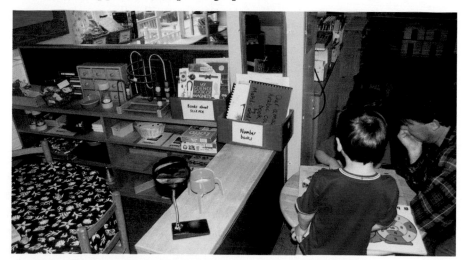

<u>Photo 29</u>

49

Children will not become creative if they are too anxious to settle and focus and develop their own ideas. The success of making the ball go along the wire without touching it or the action of threading some beads can calm children and they are then in a state to go and quietly find something that leads them into creativity. In the same way, looking at beetles and ants and spiders and stones and grass and flowers under the magnifier helps children (and adults) to concentrate and become alert to detail in ways which help creativity along.

Adults, writers in particular, often say that if they make a cup of tea or tidy up a bit, they can feel themselves developing focus on an idea. For them, the comfortable well-established routine seems to free the mind so that they begin to see the idea more clearly. Then they get into a state of mind where they can think more creatively.

Different personalities mean children have different styles of arriving

Some children burst through the doors when they arrive, going straight through the indoors area and out to the garden. They seem to need to move very freely before they settle into a creative focus. Other children flit from area to area, as if doing an audit of what is available. Others go straight to their favourite place, finding it to be an important start to the session. Some need their parent, carer or a member of staff (usually their key person) with them when they do this. Some don't. Some look for their friend, and become unsettled if he or she is absent that day.

All of these factors will influence the creativity of a child. The more we can tune into the way a child arrives in the setting, the better we can help.

Toddlers in the group setting

A two-year-old potters into the area, and wants to try just about everything. He finds himself in the home area first. He finds a frying pan and a wooden spoon. When one of the older children joins him, he gives her the pan. She shows him how to pretend to fry something on the stove. He is not interested in the symbolic side of pretending to cook, and this shows in his decision to go to the next-door area and try the mixtures table (photographs 30, 31 and 32).

Photo 30

Photo 31

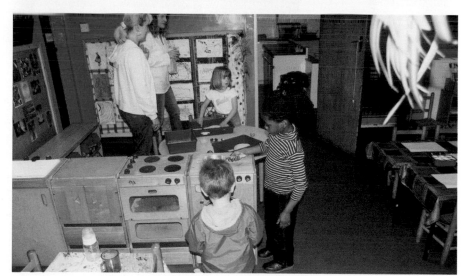

Photo 32

He is a typical toddler. He sees what he wants: the seed tray full of something, and he reaches for a small strainer and puts it into the tray the older girl is using. He does what he wants, because he does not understand that she regards that seed tray as hers whilst she is using the area! She politely restrains him and gives him a sieve, like hers, at the suggestion of a helpful adult. The adult also suggests that he might use another tray. However, he likes to be near her, so the answer is to move the tray next to the older girl. He then uses the small sieve with great concentration. He sieves into the tray, and also onto the floor (photographs 33 to 38).

Photo 33

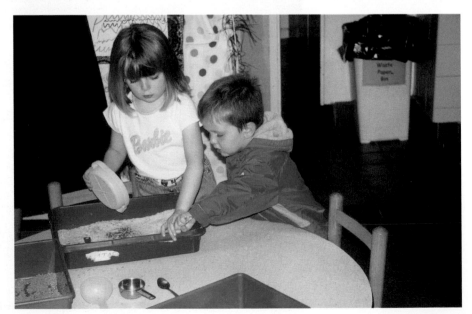

Photo 34

Toddlers often come with their older brothers and sisters, and are often unwilling to leave. Many settings now take children from 2 to 5 years of age. This has huge implications for the way in which the learning environment needs to be set up. There will need to be thought given to the development of the child. The requirements of toddlers and children with special educational and complex needs are often similar. The materials offered will be similar, but need to be offered so that the children can use them without frustration for either adults or children.

Photo 35

Photo 36

If this little boy were to stay he could be directed to use the sieve outdoors in a sand tray or in the sand pit, or on a mat for the purpose

53

Photo 37

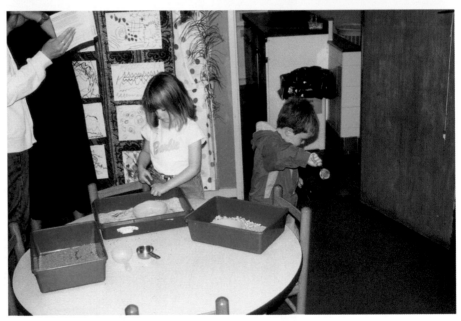

Photo 38

on the floor. There are, in this setting, plenty of opportunities for him where he can focus and learn about the properties of materials in ways that are appropriate for him. Other children are able to use materials at their level but might need some protection or support in developing strategies to divert or re-route children like this little boy, who may unwittingly destroy their ideas and creations-in-the-making because they do not yet understand creativity in action.

Having had a positive experience with mixtures, the little boy then goes exploring to the next room. He plays the drum and the large

<u>Photo 39</u>

xylophone, and then plays the piano with the stick. Then he is taken home, his mother having settled his sister in (photograph 39).

Dressing-up clothes

Squalid dressing-up areas are unhygienic and depressing, and are badly used by the children. They should be tempting areas, which children can't wait to use. Clothes should be easy to hang up, with clear places for hats, bags, shoes and jewellery (photographs 40–44).

<u>Photo 40</u>

Photo 41

Photo 42

Photo 43

Photo 44

Clothes should be simple and have suggestion rather than rigid designation of role in the costume. Expensive dressing-up clothes from catalogues are usually too definite about the character they represent to be used for a range of stories and characters. There is nothing like simple trousers, shift tops, skirts and capes as a basic wardrobe. Children are drawn towards interesting fabrics and patterns, and appreciate some changes so that boredom does not set in.

VARIATIONS OF A BASIC TUNIC

FOLD

Cut a hole

JOIN TOGETHER
(by sewing, tapes, Velcro, etc.)

BASIC TUNIC

Gathered at shoulders

Belt

ANKLE LENGTH

FRILLY MATERIAL

In this chapter we have taken a preview of how the learning environment indoors is set up before the arrival of the children and their families. We have also noted that there will be different ways of coming into the setting, reflecting the personality of each child. We have looked at some but not all areas of provision, but the principles and practical strategies outlined are part of a holistic approach, and so apply to all areas indoors and in the garden.

CHAPTER 5
CREATING AN ENVIRONMENT
– INTO THE GARDEN

Just outside the door

We saw in the last chapter that children vary in the way in which they make the daily transition from home and journey into the group setting. Some seem to come through the door and positively burst into action, often heading straight for the garden, the adult standing by supportively, without constraining their freedom of movement. Other children meander about when they arrive, as if they are waiting to see what's on offer. This, we have seen, is particularly typical of younger children and toddlers. After all, they have not yet built up enough life experience to know what, out of all the rich choices, they find most interesting and satisfying. They need to go exploring, and to 'find something of interest' (Carr, 1999).

There are children who like to be with an adult and don't settle easily unless they can read a book or do something quiet and focused together with their parent, carer or one of the staff (photograph 45). They often stay indoors for a bit (photographs 46 and 47). Others just appreciate having an adult nearby; the mere presence of an adult gives them sufficient security. There are children who like to stay indoors at first, and there are children who like to be outdoors at first.

In a well prepared learning environment, in either home care or a group setting, children are able to choose what is best for them as they settle in their own individual way into a day of developing, learning and hopefully being creative. In the home and group settings in this book, children's creativity is being cultivated to the full. We saw in an earlier chapter that in order to be creative, children need both to feel part of things and to feel that they are a separate person with their own ideas.

Photo 45

Photo 46

Photo 47

It is important to set up both the indoor and outdoor areas with these different personalities in mind, so that every child will feel comfortable about using both rooms and the outside area. Children must feel a sense of belonging and that they are themselves, in order that their creativity can develop.

In one of the settings, the first areas of provision that children will see as they go outside are:

* the office (photographs 48 and 49);
* the table with a small construction kit (photograph 50);
* a cosy place to look at books (photograph 50);
* the self-service drinks table (photograph 51);
* the Wellington boots and waterproof clothing trolley (photograph 51).

Photo 48

Photo 49

Photo 50

Photo 51

These are all areas of provision which the children can readily access. They are in a line along the immediate outside of the building. Children appreciating adult company or feeling a need for the security of sitting and doing something familiar will be likely to use the office and construction kit. Children needing larger-scale physical action might note the waterproof wear on the trolley and surge on outwards to run about before deciding what to do. This is not unusual for children who have been constrained in the freedom of their movement in a small home with no garden or after travelling in a car. Most of the children attending the settings in this book are very local, living in flats.

Children might also be noting for later use the wooden guttering and poles from which they can make waterfalls and gushing, spurting and moving water. These are all signals to the children that they can get messy and wet (photograph 52).

Photo 52

Further into the garden

As they adventure further into the garden, they find a challenging climbing frame, tyres, a row of beads nailed to the posts (photographs 53, 54 and 55).

Photo 53

<u>Photo 54</u>

<u>Photo 55</u>

There is plenty of space to run about unconstrained and also places which challenge the direction in which the child runs (straight or circular running) and which require more co-ordination. For example, at the bottom of the garden the concentric circles are well used by children going round and round at speed without falling off each circle as they move from one to the next in challenging themselves (photograph 56).

63

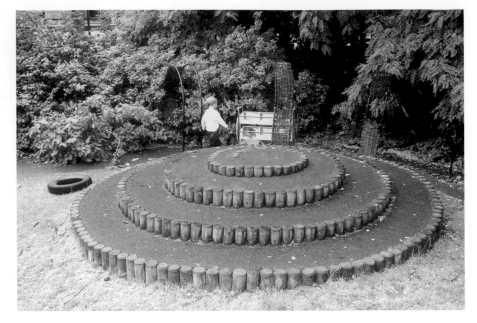

Photo 56

As children move further into the garden, with their friends, with or without an adult, they encounter another table with books, a sandpit shaded from too much sun, wind or rain, and quiet places to sit, such as the miniature Greek amphitheatre, where stories are told and dances and songs take place whenever the weather permits in group times at the end of the session (photographs 57 and 58).

There are pictures and labels of the typical wildlife found in the well-placed bushes in the middle and at the bottom of the garden. Children are often found pausing between play episodes, when they are in transition to their next focus, looking with quiet, focused interest at these (photographs 59 and 60).

Photo 57

Photo 58

Photo 59

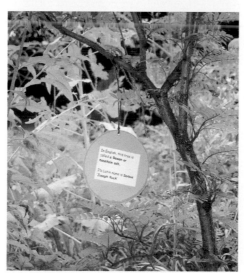

Photo 60

Children who are well established in the setting know that once the to and fro of the start of the day is ended, staff will help them to take out the wheeled vehicles and the large hollow blocks. Doing this together saves the staff some physical energy, because the children help. It also encourages the children to think about how they might use the different vehicles, and in developing their ideas they move into a creative mode (photographs 61 and 62).

Photo 61

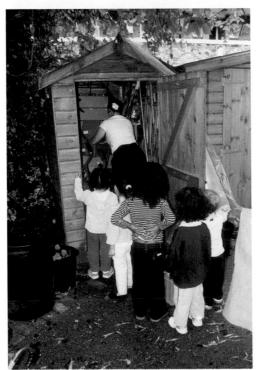

Photo 62

Books, books everywhere

Wherever the children go indoors and outdoors they find books. The books are relevant to the area of material provision they support, and also pick up on current interests of clusters of children or individual children. For example, there are books about art in the painting area, and books about puzzles and games in that area (photograph 63).

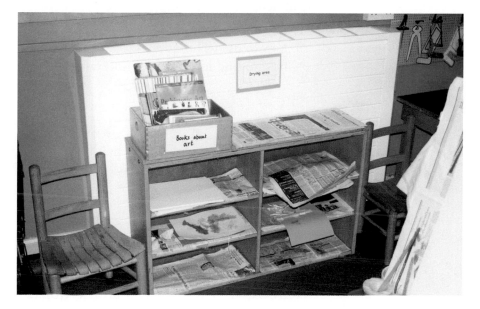

Photo 63

Each room also has a story area with books in it. This can also be used for wooden unit block play in one room (photograph 64) and for stories with props in the other room (see photographs 46 and 47 earlier in the chapter).

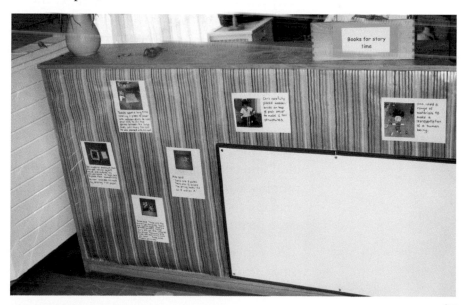

Photo 64

Seeing other people's ideas for stories, songs and poems (fiction) and factual books (non-fiction) helps children to see new and creative possibilities. They use what they find, rearrange, alter, adapt ideas that other people have, for their own stories, models, constructions, dances, music, paintings and drawings and scientific theorising.

In later chapters we shall find that, time and again, books are very important in cultivating creativity. They help us to explore with the children:

✳ how to do things;
✳ how to use techniques;
✳ how to find information: for example, about volcanoes.

What have we found out about cultivating creativity so far?

Creativity is not a gift that we are born with.

Creativity is part of everyone's development and learning.

Unless it is helped along and supported, actively encouraged and cultivated, the possibilities for it to develop can be extinguished or constrained.

We have found three kinds of creativity:

1. everyday creativity;
2. specialist creativity;
3. world-shattering creativity.

Most creativity is of the first kind, so that is the main focus of this book. Very little is of the last kind. Specialists, however, are very influential in the impact they have on our daily lives through their creativity. We sometimes know their names, but often we don't.

Some people are very good at interpreting other people's creative ideas. Good performers do this. Other people are better at both creating ideas and taking them to fruition, turning them into creations. Creative people use their own ideas when they do this. Of course, there are often overlaps: for example, when the creator and performer are one and the same person.

Creative people do not have to be difficult and temperamental. This is not a condition that is necessary in order for someone to be creative. Most creative people are well balanced, which is why they are able to develop their ideas and thoughts sufficiently to carry them through to fruition, with a creation as the result. Jung, the famous psychologist, thought that being neurotic is 'the most formidable obstacle to creation' (in Howkins, 2003: 5).

We find creativity of different kinds. Sometimes it is entirely in the way we use our senses and movements. At other times, it is in the way we develop and use symbols of all kinds. Symbols stand for something else. Those who, for one reason or another, cannot develop symbolic creativity can still be creative in ways which use the senses and movements. Creativity develops in layers.

> Creative people have new ideas, but this doesn't make them revolutionaries. It means they are using their adaptive human intelligence. Seeing new ways of doing things is part of intelligent behaviour. It is central to creativity. Creativity is a high level aspect of thinking because it shows depth of:
> ☐ process (developing the idea inside your mind); and
> ☐ product (outward creation emerging from the idea).

What has setting up the environment got to do with cultivating creativity?

Creativity doesn't just happen. Just as babies do not learn to speak or sign unless they are spoken to, in the same way, babies, toddlers and young children do not develop creativity without help. It might be argued that it is more important to learn to speak or sign than it is to be a creative person. In some ways this is true. People who cannot communicate with others are in great difficulty. Neither is thinking at a sophisticated level possible without language. However, creativity takes the commonplace out of life and makes life satisfying and fulfilling. It develops the ability for thinking, because it is about developing ideas and hatching them into creations. To do this, thinking has to be flexible, has to adapt, be able to rearrange ideas and to follow ideas through without losing them on the way. Creativity is hard work.

People who carry creative experiences inside them live more fully. They have more control over what happens to them because they have dispositions towards life which make them full of adventure, and they both solve and generate problems in order to find better ways of doing things. They are less likely to be passive people who depend on others to do their thinking for them, waiting for instructions and anxious about whether they are pleasing their instructors or angry at their lack of personal power.

We can see that when the children enter the learning environments in this book, whether in home care or group settings, those environments have been set up to cultivate their creativity (photographs 65, 66).

Photo 65

Photo 66

So far in the book, we have only glimpsed some of the learning environment indoors and outdoors. We have not yet looked at everything on offer to the children. We shall do this in future chapters of the book.

BUT EVEN AS THEY ARRIVE EACH DAY, THE CHILDREN:
- [ ] choose and make decisions;
- [ ] find a wide range of experiences;
- [ ] are challenged with problems to solve;
- [ ] take risks and have adventures in learning;
- [ ] find a predictable, safe environment where there are clear boundaries;
- [ ] are supported by informed, highly trained staff, led by graduate-trained teachers;
- [ ] learn how to use the materials at the level appropriate for them;
- [ ] are listened to;
- [ ] are encouraged to share their emerging thoughts;
- [ ] find their creations valued and discussed with them;
- [ ] are respected when they are concentrating on an idea;
- [ ] find that adults protect their personal space when they need to focus;
- [ ] find that adults are good companions when they are finding a focus;
- [ ] are given help when they ask for it;
- [ ] are given help when they are struggling, so that they don't give up;
- [ ] are allowed to develop their own ideas, and adults don't take them over;
- [ ] are with adults who support their creative ideas;
- [ ] see that their parents are partners with the staff.

These bullet points show some of the **conditions for cultivating creativity**. The boxes in each chapter of the book help us to piece together the jigsaw that cultivates creativity. We can begin to see that although creativity is a complex part of development and learning, there are positive things we can do to cultivate it.

CHAPTER 6
INCLUDING EVERYONE – THE BEGINNINGS OF CREATIVITY

Babies – emergent creativity

There is often a view that children can be creative only when they have acquired certain techniques that enable them to make creations. There are several problems with this point of view.

First, educators who say this do not distinguish between:

* knowing about the beginnings and early emergent signs of creativity in babies or those who for one reason or another (early traumatic experiences, ill health, special educational needs, disabilities or complex needs) are later in developing their creativity;
* being creative;
* making a creation.

Their view focuses only on children's ability to make a creation that complies with conventional criteria of the culture.

Second, when this view is taken, then creativity is really seen as the way in which the child learns a craft, with the techniques needed being directly taught. The adult gives the child the skills and technical know-how, and then the child is free to be creative. This is a linear view of creativity, and suggests that a child can be creative only if they are skilled enough to make creations. It does not value the individual creativity of the child.

Third, it sees creativity as a skilled craft (usually emphasising the arts and not the humanities or sciences), as an ability to create things according to cultural expectations and requirements.

In this book a different view is taken. Creativity is thought of as an umbrella word, with three things under it, each of equal importance:

1. emergent beginnings of creativity;
2. being a creative learner (a process);
3. making creations (products).

These do not develop in a linear way, although the emergent beginnings inevitably come first. Being a creative learner is a state of mind throughout life if the beginnings are cultivated too. Some of us are more inclined to make products than others. Some of us make creative products that change the world. Some of us make creative products that show great expertise, and help knowledge and understanding to develop in important but often small ways. Some of us make everyday creative products, that increase the satisfaction and fulfilment of our lives in personal and individual ways.

Creativity in babies begins through relationships with particular people, and through non-verbal communication. It also begins with learning through the senses and the sixth sense of movement feedback (embodiment, which brings a sense of self and connectedness with others). Flo Longhorn (1988), in her pioneering work with children with complex needs, points out that a diverse range of people need a particular emphasis on multi-sensory learning at various points in their lives. These include:

* babies;
* premature babies;
* under-stimulated children (physical, emotional and intellectual neglect);
* people with failing senses (going deaf or blind);
* someone who has been in a coma;
* older people;
* people in hospital settings;
* those re-joining a community after leaving a hospital setting;
* children with specific learning difficulties;
* people undergoing therapeutic difficulties. (Longhorn, 1988: 18–19)

Through multi-sensory experiences in companionship and interactions with people they love, children develop a sense of embodiment which gives them a sense of 'me, myself and I' (DfES, 2002). The beginnings of creativity emerge in the way that very young babies see themselves as the cause of making things happen and making people behave in certain ways. Autonomy and a sense of our own agency is a crucial part of multi-sensory experience. Predicting and anticipating are a part of this.

We can encourage these glimmerings of the creative self in babies, right from the start, by helping them to see the impact of what they do.

A classic example is Magda, who is sitting in her high chair. She is given a rusk to keep her busy while her mother prepares the meal by heating it. She bangs the rusk on the tray, and pauses to listen to the different sounds – on the edge, on top, on the top of her head.

Here we see **variation** on the same action – banging.

Then she picks at the rusk, and notices how it crumbles a bit. She likes the crumbs, and drops them onto the tray. She stirs them about in a circular movement, and looks at her mother for her reaction. Her mother says, 'You're a mucky thing, aren't you? Stirring your rusk round and round! (making the action with her arm). Yes! You're a messy girl, you are!'. This is said in a jovial tone. Magda returns to her stirring gleefully.

Her mother has responded in an important way. She has called attention to the pattern Magda has made. She has shown Magda what she has done. Magda looks at the round pattern, and does it again. This encourages her to predict and anticipate the fact that a particular action leads to a particular pattern with the crumbs. Having a sense of intention, as these cause and effect relationships develop, will in the future help Magda to develop creative ideas which she will have some control over, and at times will manage to turn into creations.

Let's look at the beginnings of becoming a creative learner in more detail.

Lynne Murray and Liz Andrews show us how, in the second and third months of life, babies enjoy face-to-face play:

Face-to-face play with babies in the second and third months can seem like a musical duet, and distinct phrases when the baby's initiative is taken up by the parent who, quite unconsciously, mirrors, builds on and develops the baby's original communication. Play is intimate, and concerns nothing but the feelings and expressions of the two partners. The parents' mirroring is a very immediate way of conveying their acceptance of the baby, and it can both affirm and enrich the baby's experience. (Murray and Andrews, 2000: 52)

Time and again in this book we return to the importance of adults tuning into the child's spontaneous initiatives, efforts to communicate and intentions. Joey looks at his mother and moves as his face changes expression. When we see a baby move in a very lively way whilst looking intently at us, and perhaps cooing at us too, we need to tune in at once. We can make a 'musical duet' together. Trevarthen (1998) talks about these as early two-way conversations without words.

As these become well-established, Murray and Andrews show how the baby uses the known and familiar, predictable structure to anticipate and feel a sense of agency and control over events:

Common examples are body games, such as 'round and round the garden' or even the very simple routines, like the looming in of the partner's face to touch the baby's tummy. These may start gently, the baby quite seriously watching the partner's face; then the partner gradually helps to build up the sense of anticipation, holding the baby's gaze and monitoring her readiness throughout, using voice, facial expression and widening of the eyes to mark the imminent arrival of the final climax, when the high point of emotion is shared together. In this way, the face-to-face conversations develop from simply focusing on what the baby may be feeling or thinking, to having a definite structure and topic. (Murray and Andrews, 2000: 63)

Topics are often 'coo and boo' games and gradually, from three months typically, involve the wider world of objects, such as dummies and rattles.

Babies are born with the possibility to be both problem solvers and problem generators (Karmiloff-Smith, 1992). Both require creative learning, although generating problems emphasises this more. As we have noted in other parts of the book, learning through a multi-sensory world and from their own movements is crucial to babies. Alison Gopnik, Andrew Meltzoff and Patricia Kuhl describe this sense of embodiment in the developing sense of self (me, myself and I) and suggest that:

There is nothing more personal, more part of you, than this internal sense you have of your own body, your expressions and movements, your aches and tickles. And yet from the time we are born, we seem to link this deeply personal self to the bodily movements of other people, movements we can only see and not feel. Nature ingeniously gives us a jump start on the Other Minds problem. We know, quite directly, that we are like other people and they are like us. (Gopnik et al., 1999: 30)

Babies' sense of embodiment connects with the sense that other people are like them. They have a sense of connection with other people, which bypasses spoken or signed language, and opens up the beginnings of creative learning.

Predicting, anticipating and controlling – the beginnings of creativity

One of the ways in which we know that babies have made an important start in realising they are creative learners is observing their joy, typically after the first two months of their lives, in being able to predict, anticipate and control. They revel in their sense of agency, through which they realise there is a connection between what they do and how people react. They widen this exciting realisation and begin to apply it to objects too. They become fascinated by novelty. It is as if they are asking themselves the question, 'Do people and things always react in the same way when I do this or that?'.

There are many psychological tests with babies which are based on the look of surprise when a baby's prediction does not turn out as expected (Goswami, 1998). If things do turn out as expected time and time again, then the baby becomes bored and moves to something else.

Novelty and variations on a theme – emergent creativity

Novelty and variations on a theme are at the heart of the baby becoming a creative learner, but it is the baby who needs to control this, because only the baby has a sense of what will happen. The adult does not know what the baby's predictions are. The adult can help by being a tuned-in partner in the play. Offering to play and being sensitive to the baby's mood is important at times. Responding to the baby's spontaneous requests to play is important at other times.

The beginnings of creative learning emerge out of the ideas babies have from birth. Gopnik *et al.* (1999) suggest that they use these to learn more, elaborating what they know in the light of their experiences with people and the physical world they are introduced to by people.

We can see how our knowledge emerges from the ideas we start out with, our ability to learn and our interactions with other people. (Gopnik et al., 1999: 206)

They point out that in evolutionary terms, the dangers linked with babies, toddlers and young children being explorers are offset by the benefits of the beginnings of a life-long possibility for creative, thinking, autonomous learning. As they develop their sense of embodied self and being an active agent in producing causes for things to happen, and observing the effects of their actions on people and objects, they learn about the way things disappear, and how to classify and organise what they know into concepts that help them to think more deeply.

By the time they can sit, babies:

will systematically examine a new object with every sense they have at their command (including taste, of course). (Gopnik et al., 1999: 88)

By the end of their first year they typically vary what they do with an object, perhaps tapping gently, then banging fiercely. As toddlers, they look for the unexpected in an object, as if fascinated, and sort things into piles which have, amazingly, to the tuned-in observer, some consistent logic in them (Gopnik *et al.*, 1999). This kind of creative thinking is significant for human learning. Other animals cannot manage creative thinking of this depth.

Cultural variations

Of course, as we would expect, there are cultural variations and great diversities in the kinds of creative learning that develop in babies, toddlers and young children, because people in different cultures and contexts cultivate creativity (or don't cultivate creativity) in very different ways.

For example, Korean parents talking with their babies emphasise problem-solving, such as how to get an out-of-reach toy, whereas English-speaking parents talk about the categories of objects more, such as, 'Here's your cup'. But by the age of two years, Korean children understand all about the categories of objects and English-speaking toddlers understand the actions of people and objects.

Babies seem to learn about the external world in much the way they learn about other minds. They start out with some crucial assumptions, assumptions that seem to be built in. But, just as important, they are endowed with powerful abilities to learn, and even more powerful motivations. (Gopnik et al., 1999: 91)

Movement patterns and creative beginnings

John Matthews (2003) mentions the repertoire of movement patterns (schemas) available to babies, which become elaborated as the baby begins to experiment and receive feedback from people and objects.

Joel, at just over six months, is lying on his stomach on a purple carpet. He regurgitates some milk onto the carpet in front of him, presenting a contrasting white, circular patch before his eyes. He reaches his fingers into this irresistible visual target and makes a scratching movement. He hears his fingers scratching into the carpet and seems to be interested in the changes he is causing to take place. (Matthews, 2003: 52)

Gradually, babies begin to realise that they can make marks with paint, crayons, milk on their food tray. Earlier in the chapter, we saw how Magda made a trajectory pathway through the pile of crumbs on her high-chair tray.

We find the beginnings of creativity in the way babies explore:
- [ ] A sense of embodiment – movement feedback
- [ ] Seeing others move, and realising they are people who move like me
- [ ] Face-to-face interactions between baby and a loved person
- [ ] Predictable forms of play – tickle games or coo and boo responses
- [ ] Cause and effect – I did that
- [ ] Does that happen every time I do that? Predicting and anticipating
- [ ] I can make things happen and people do things too – sense of agency
- [ ] Variations and novelty

Special educational needs, disabilities and complex needs – looking for signs of emergent creativity

Throughout this book there are examples of children engaged in creative thinking and acts of creation. Amongst these are children with special educational needs and disabilities. They are not easy to spot, because when children feel included they do not stand out. They belong and are part of their community.

The submarine and the viking ship

When he was about seven years of age, Chris made a Viking boat out of coloured pipe cleaners. It happened quite quickly. He had been learning about Vikings at school, but this happened during the holidays. He was given the packet of pipe-cleaners as a gift, and he picked his way through them, and then began twisting them with intense concentration. The next thing anyone knew, he had made a Viking ship.

Children are sometimes a little taken aback by their creations. It is as if they can hardly believe what they have created. He sat looking at it. The adult did not say, 'What is it?' This might have been rather deflating for him. Instead she said, 'That's an intricate construction. I'd love to know more about it'. He told her it was a Viking ship. She could see this at once, and she admired the different features. She put it in her glass-fronted bookcase in front of some books. It stayed there for years. It is still there now! It is valued, appreciated and treasured.

Photo 67

David watched this scene with interest. He is younger than his brother. Four years later, when he was nine years old, he arrived at the house with a huge construction made of wood. It was painted grey. His father had helped him to make it – holding the wood still and making sure the nails were well placed to bang them in with the hammer without bending. He announced, 'I made you a submarine'. He moved swiftly to the glass fronted book-case, clearly expecting a place to be found for it. A shelf was quickly cleared of books, and the submarine just fitted onto it. He looked at it with pride, and muttered, with deep satisfaction, 'Boat, like my brother'.

For four years, he had been incubating the idea. He needed time for the idea to take root, to gather his thoughts, to find a form for them, and then to take it into a tangible shape as a submarine. It took four years to:

* prepare;
* incubate;
* illuminate;
* hatch.

It is easy to underestimate the time it takes for children to develop a creative idea, especially those children with disabilities. At a dance lesson at RNIB Redhill College, attended by Further Education students with complex needs, of which visual disability is dominant, it was evident that the need to take the time to cultivate creativity was built into the way the timetable had been developed. The dance ideas were developed with staff tuning into the individual dance ideas of each student. One student loved to put her arms out, as in second position ballet, and really used the music to give expression to her movement. Staff had helped her to decide where she should place herself, when she should use her dance motif, and when she should walk across the dance floor. Another student twirled across the room, rotating with his arm out.

Including everyone in creativity

Stuart Jackson is a student of the RNIB college. Since 1994 he has been attending the life skills programme in literacy, numeracy, mobility, Braille and self-help skills. In 2003 he joined the S.T.E.P. (Saburo Teshigawara Education Project) and toured with the dance company in Helsinki and other countries, finishing with a performance at the Sadlers Wells Theatre. This example highlights the point made in the first chapter, that anyone can be creative. The kind of dance improvisations he had been encouraged to develop at the RNIB College were seen by the director of the dance company, who had invited him to join the company.

It is important to recognise that creativity is possible in every human being. Music, dance and the visual arts are areas where this often emerges, because these do not depend on verbal or signed languages. This does not mean that these forms of the arts are easier than the humanities or sciences. But they are different. They do not need words. They open up important areas of ourselves which help us to live very fully.

Children with special educational needs, disabilities and complex needs have the same requirements as other children in relation to how adults can help them to cultivate their creativity. They need:
- [ ] People who believe they can be creative
- [ ] A supportive setting and learning environment
- [ ] To be encouraged to develop their play
- [ ] A consistent environment with a rich range of materials
- [ ] Experiences offered which are interesting to them
- [ ] To be encouraged to make decisions and choices
- [ ] To be given personal space to develop their ideas
- [ ] To be offered music, dance, artistic experiences in particular because these do not depend on verbal or signed languages
- [ ] To be offered song, poetry, story, and real first-hand experiences of food preparation, shopping etc.
- [ ] To be talked with (not at) such that the adult shows genuine interest in what the child communicates

One area that tends to be challenging for some (but not by any means all) children with disabilities is imagination. Peter McKellar (1957) sees the imagination as the way that we rearrange our past experiences and knowledge in new and often rather fascinating ways. In order to do this, we form an image in our minds – a mental image. This can be:

* auditory – sound;
* visual – sight;
* tactile – touch;

* olfactory – smell;
* taste;
* kinaesthetic – movement feedback.

Children with disabilities may have difficulty with some of these senses, but they use the ones they have. Robert Orr (2003) suggests that the sense of smell is very important for children with complex needs.

Becoming imaginative – it's all in the head

Mental images are an important part of developing the ability to be a symbol user. When children represent things, perhaps draw a digger, as Matthew did, or the Mary Rose ship, as Kit did, use their past experiences and externalise them, instead of keeping them inside as private images.

We do not always find out the mental imagery of children, precisely because it is inside them! But this doesn't mean that it isn't there.

Another important aspect of becoming a symbol user is **imitation**. This is another way of rearranging our experiences. Imitation is not copying. When we copy we do exactly the same as the person or thing we copy. When we imitate, we take an idea and incorporate it into our own ideas, using it as a resource.

Again, children with special educational needs, disabilities and complex needs are often able to imitate, taking other people's ideas and making them their own.

Pretending is more difficult, but often role play is helpful here. Anne, parent of Megan, a ten-year-old with learning difficulties, found that her daughter kept having temper tantrums when she arrived home, tired, at the end of a day spent in her early years setting. She suggested that she and her daughter act a story called, 'Coming home'. She offered to be the 'little girl', and invited Megan to be the 'mother'. Megan agreed, with enthusiasm. They had an enjoyable time deciding on their costumes and dressed up as their characters. The 'mother' talked, imitating Anne's way of talking, and the 'child' had a full-scale temper tantrum.

Megan looked aghast. She was shocked. It helped her to see how her mother felt. She began to look at what was happening from her mother's viewpoint. Megan began to develop the play, making further events in the story, such as being bad-tempered at meal times, or going to bed, or wanting sweets when out shopping. She couldn't manage to play such scenarios with dolls or small world. She could manage it only if she had her mother playing with her in partnership and could direct Anne in the play.

Anne did not try to force her into small world play or doll play, because she could see that the play would deepen into free-flow play if she allowed herself to become Megan's play prop and carry out her own creative 'script'.

We often find that children with learning difficulties and disabilities develop pretend play much later, sometimes, as we see with Megan, many years later than most children. It is important therefore to continue to give them the kind of learning environment which encourages its development.

Piaget thought that in order for symbol use to develop, children need to:
- ❐ **make images in their minds;**
- ❐ **imitate (rather than copy);**
- ❐ **pretend in their play.**

In this book we keep emphasising the way that free-flowing play, with its flexible, mobile, adaptive features, contributes to creative ideas developing. As images become increasingly mobile and connected, then deeper layers of creative thinking become possible. When creative thinking is well under way, then creations might begin to form. The encouraging thing from the point of view of children with complex needs is that the ability to pretend is not essential to creative thinking. Symbolic creativity is one kind of creativity, but not the only one. Children can be original in other ways too.

Having an intention

This is where it is useful to look at babies to see the kinds of developments into the processes of being creative that are there before symbol use has developed. In the strict and pure sense, the creator has to intend to create something, but it seems to be the case that, in its beginnings, the move into being creative might simply mean having an awareness that something is happening which they want to happen; they can't express it in words or signs. We have seen in an earlier part of the book that the glimmerings of having an intention are part of the development into being creative.

Abraham Maslow writes about having what he calls 'peak experiences'. He thought that these moments brought together creativeness and a sense of self.

PEAK EXPERIENCES (Maslow, 1973: 59) BRING TOGETHER:
- ☐ Being creative (the processes involved)
- ☐ A sense of self

Being a creative learner is preceded by signs of the emergent beginnings of creativity. It is a long process. Babies are at the beginning of it, and so are some of the children we work or live with who have special educational needs, disabilities and complex needs, or who are recovering from illnesses or traumatic experiences.

CHAPTER 7
CULTIVATING CREATIVITY IN TODDLERS

We have seen in earlier chapters that creativity is about both being a separate individual and feeling connected to others, with a sense of belonging to a group and culture. Children who are helped to develop their unique and personal creations will also be participating in the cultural context in which they grow up. In this way they will come to know themselves as creative people, and also be competent in interpreting and using the creations which become the conventions of the culture.

Toddlers are at an exciting point in their lives, because they are beginning to realise that they are separate and different from other people, although their need to belong is strong. Like teenagers, they are fiercely independent, but they also need support and guidance.

They are also beginning to become symbol users. This means that they are beginning to realise that they can make one thing stand for another, whether or not it is present.

Personal symbols and creativity

Throughout their lives, creative people develop their own personal symbols. They never lose the ability to do this. People who are not creative either never develop this aspect of living to any great extent or lose the ability as early childhood fades. This leads to the living of commonplace lives, such as Isadora Duncan described. This means that their lives are not deeply satisfying in the way that they could be.

When toddlers are helped to develop their personal symbols, they find this very exciting. For example, in a group setting a group of two- and three-year-olds had visited the local shops, and one of the children had fallen in love with the adult's rucksack into which the shopping had been put. The staff decided to set up a supermarket in the room. They had a bag area, where children could choose what to carry their shopping in. They put out tins and wooden beads, and scrunched up newspaper for the children to buy pretend vegetables and fruit.

One of the children had been fascinated with the credit card, and the way it was swiped at the computer at the pay desk. The adult made some cards which were the same size as the credit cards, and asked the children to sign them, showing them her credit card. This really took off, with all the children wanting credit cards to 'sign' with scribble. This then led to children needing wallets and purses in which to put their credit cards. One child wanted some money. A box of counters was found in the cupboard, and children could use this as pretend money.

Within minutes the room and outdoor area were swarming with children with bags containing purses, money and credit cards. There was a great deal of opening and shutting bags, and walking about. The most popular bags were the rucksacks.

The pay desk was hectic with activity. Toddlers love queues. They also enjoyed taking the supermarket baskets and filling them with 'shopping' and then unloading them at the pay desk. There was also a collection of paper bags into which children could put their pretend fruit and vegetables. The adult, Judy, based herself at the pay desk, in order to support the 'shopkeeper' in putting the goods into plastic carrier bags and swiping the credit cards with gusto. The cash register was a plastic replica bought from a toy catalogue and kept for situations such as this.

Observing the way in which children developed their person symbols during this free-flow play scenario was illuminating. One child chose to wear a hat. Another selected the pink rucksack and walked around the garden with it on her back, pushing her 'baby' in the pram. When she came inside she was allowed to bring the pushchair, and delighted in putting her purchases on the rack under the chair.

Toddlers need adult support in developing their creativity

As always, the adult support was of central importance in cultivating the creative ideas of these children. If the little girl had not been allowed to bring the pushchair inside, although there is a rule that vehicles may not be brought indoors, her play and the creative ideas that were part of it would have faded and vanished.

If adults had moved in on the children's play too much, they would have turned it into their story with the children as actors in it. Instead they cultivated the children's creative ideas by giving them open-ended props as suggestions, such as the cards for credit cards, newspaper balls as fruit and vegetables, bags and a commercial toy computer cash register.

When children are just beginning to develop symbolic creative ideas, they need props to help them sustain their ideas. Toddlers are often not too fussy about how realistic these look, as we saw with the credit cards and newspaper food. However, they do like to use real things as well, such as the rucksacks. These seem to serve as realistic anchors to their creative ideas as they free-flow play. This might be why they are such fierce possessors of some objects.

For toddlers, losing a play prop means losing the creative moment in the free-flow play. Certainly fierce fights developed over the supermarket baskets, until more arrived from other rooms in the setting. The creative ideas in the play of toddlers can be quickly destroyed when disputes over property break out. Sharing and taking turns are unreasonable requests on the part of adults in such situations. With team work, more props can usually be provided. There are recurring themes in children's play. Food preparation and related subjects are by far the most popular play scenarios amongst toddlers across the world. If adults plan resources with this in mind, potential fights can be kept to a minimum. Bags, hats, props to symbolise money, paper bags, prams and a cash register are likely to be needed very regularly in a group of toddlers.

Lauren (eighteen months) enjoys playing shops at home with her three-year-old sister, Kim-Anh. Her sister initiates the play and she willingly follows. Kim-Anh decides that Lauren needs a shopping basket, and so she takes her by the hand to find one (photograph 68). Lauren, who probably doesn't realise that she is 'playing shops', takes the basket with the objects Kim-Anh puts into it, into the other room as directed by her sister (photograph 69). She looks pleased to hold the basket. Kim-Anh sits her down next to the cash desk and encourages her to check out her shopping. She swipes each item that she takes from Lauren.

Older children are often the ones who introduce toddlers to dramatic play that contains the beginnings of creative thinking in

Photo 68

Photo 69

Photo 70

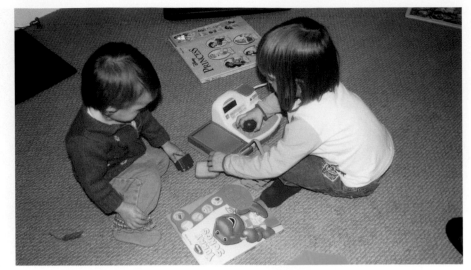

Photo 71

relation to literature and stories. Lauren is happy to take part in the shop play, and once she is at the checkout counter is a very willing participant. She knows that you have to give objects to the person sitting at the desk and that you get them back to put in your basket. However, it is evident from her body movement and involvement in what she is doing (Laevers, 1994) that she enjoys the food preparation play more. This is often the first kind of role play that toddlers actively take part in (photograph 72).

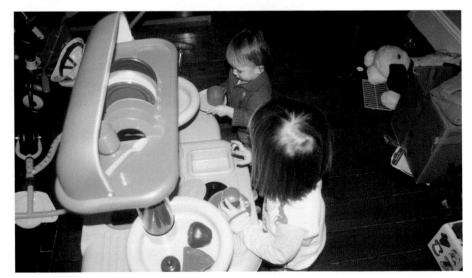

Photo 72

A recent arrival, fast taking over from the traditional telephone play of toddlers, is mobile phone play (Christiansen, 2002). Lauren needs a realistic prop, and shows that she knows you have to press buttons and then listen. Phones are cultural artefacts of great importance for modern toddlers growing up in the UK (photographs 73 and 74).

Photo 73

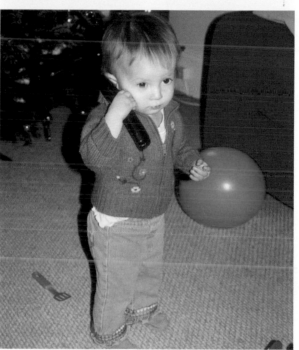

Photo 74

Lauren also plays with dolls, and shows her doll to her mother and then her father. Toddlers delight in giving and then taking back objects. Interestingly, she seems to understand that in order to play with the doll's house she needs a doll small enough to fit into its rooms, so she rejects the larger doll and finds a smaller one. She is more interested in putting the doll in and out than anything else. She is not yet ready to make her own story about the doll who lives in the house (photographs 75, 76 and 77).

Photo 75

Photo 76

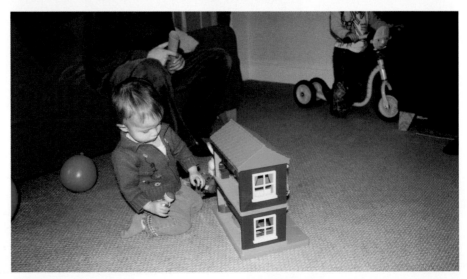

Photo 77

Nevertheless, it is remarkable to think that she has only recently started to walk, talk and pretend, and yet she is already showing a range of creative thinking in early form.

❋ She is beginning to learn about playing shops with her sister;
❋ she is confident about pretending to prepare food;
❋ she is confident about pretending to use a mobile phone;
❋ she knows some dolls fit in dolls' houses.

Her parents, without consciously realising it, are putting into action the strategies in the box below, and showing her the sensitivity that is crucial to her creative development. Her father realises she is tiring after her burst of food preparation play, shop play and doll's house play, and encourages her to have a quiet time sharing a book with him.

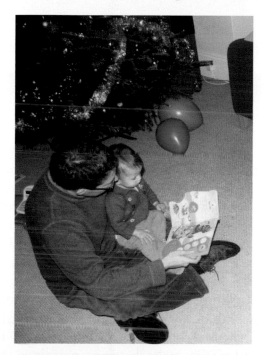

Photo 78

CULTIVATING CREATIVITY IN TODDLERS
☐ **Showing genuine interest**
☐ **Getting down low to communicate with them**
☐ **Giving them eye contact**
☐ **Talking to them, but respecting their personal space**
☐ **Showing them how to do things when they are stuck**
☐ **Protecting them from being overwhelmed by their older sibling when necessary**
☐ **Recognising that pretending is energy-sapping**
☐ **Providing a book to share when they have had enough**
☐ **Having a cuddle**
☐ **Being sensitive to their interests and moods**

CHAPTER 8
HOW ADULTS CAN HELP CREATIVE IDEAS TO BE CULTIVATED

Creativity doesn't come from nowhere

So far in this book we have dwelt on the importance of offering a rich range of material provision which will give children plentiful experiences that they may then use as the germ of a creative idea. Some of these creative thoughts may then develop, by means of what is called creative processing, into an idea that is expressed overtly. This is called a creation. Again, having a wide range of material provision is of great importance because we are all so different in our modes of taking creative ideas to fruition. Some like to dance their ideas, some to make them into musical expressions. Some form scientific theories, or mathematical patterns, whilst others write poems and stories, make drawings, paintings, collages and sculptures and pottery.

We need to remember that babies, toddlers and young children have not yet lived for very long. They need to be offered life experience because, as we saw earlier in the book, creativity doesn't come from nowhere. It feeds off our experiences. It depends on them in order for creative ideas to develop.

We also need to remember that we will probably see more creative ideas developing than come to fruition as acts of creation. In this respect, children and adults are rather similar. However, we are all helped to be more creative, both in the ideas we have and in the likelihood that our creative ideas will become externalised into creations, if other people support and encourage our creative thinking.

Margaret Donaldson (1992: 256), in her book *Human Minds*, emphasises the importance of adults in children's learning. She warns against extreme approaches, saying children need to spend time with adults who 'avoid being bound to a single point of view'. Those who are what she calls extremely child-centred, or on the other hand extremely culture-centred, disadvantage children in different ways:

If education is culture-centred, then conformity, decorum and the conveying of information are overvalued, and there is an underestimation of the child's ingenuity, imagination and initiative. There is also an underestimation of the human capacity for defiance and rejection and of the dire effects of boredom.

... the main risk of the child-centred extreme is that of overestimating children's powers of self-direction and the validity of their judgements, while underestimating not only their need for systematic, well-thought-out help but also their willingness to receive this help if it is not forced upon them in insensitive ways. (Donaldson, 1992: 256–57)

CULTIVATING CREATIVITY

☐ The provision of experiences which feed creative ideas

☐ Being offered a wide range of materials through which to express creative ideas

☐ Being helped to learn the skills and techniques that are needed in order to use a particular medium or material on a 'need to' basis

☐ Organising a learning environment which provokes, in many ways, the 'need to' learn skills and techniques useful for lifelong creativity

☐ Being given the time and personal space, as well as the discussions and respectful help where needed, to develop an interest

☐ Being helped in the way that is needed at that moment to develop an interest

---

The English Foundation Stage document, *Curriculum Guidance for the Foundation Stage* (QCA/DfES, 2000) emphasises the importance of identifying and developing children's interests. It also emphasises that it is important to give children what they need as we build on their interests. Children learn more and with deeper quality if they find things that interest them as individuals. This is not therefore a sentimental or romantic view of learning. It actually maximises the most effective ways of learning.

The provision of experiences and materials which feed into creative ideas and processes

As the learning gets under way in the homes and group settings in this book, there is a great emphasis on the experiences the children are offered and helped to get the most from by identifying and cultivating their interests.

Because children are free to be selective, make choices and come to decisions, they become very focused. This cultivates creativity.

Photo 79

Photo 80

Children are to be found in all corners and areas of the indoor and outdoor learning environment. Some choose to cook or sew (photographs 79–80). For these choices they often need adult support. Perhaps because the techniques are particularly challenging for physical and mental co-ordination when learning to cook or sew, we see less creativity here. However, children often have creative ideas about sewing and cooking, which, if adults were on the look-out for, they could help the children to develop into creations. There is a tendency to insist on the result of the cooking or sewing looking like a perfect product, but sometimes a less perfect result might have involved the child in more creative thinking.

Sharing a book with an adult is an area of provision where there is an emphasis on telling and retelling a story. However, here again children will often introduce their own creative thoughts around the text. This is why sharing stories one to one or in very small groups, where there can be plenty of discussion and encouragement of the children's ideas, cultivates creativity.

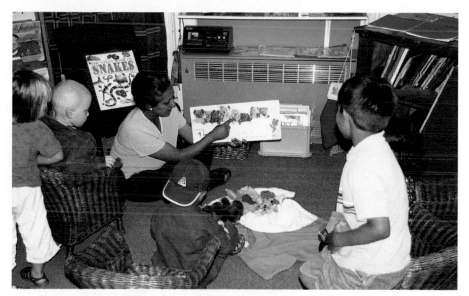

Photo 81

There are other areas of provision where adults have a greater expectation that the children will have their own creative ideas. The workshop area is one of these. The woodwork bench, sandpit, wooden block play and small world are others.

There are two children busy at the woodwork bench. They each have ideas they are working on, although it is quite likely that they won't be able to express these in words. It is easier to explain something after you have created it than it is before you make it. It can be very damaging to the idea to try and pin it down into concrete words before it has been developed and turned into a creation. We often don't know

Photo 82

Photo 83

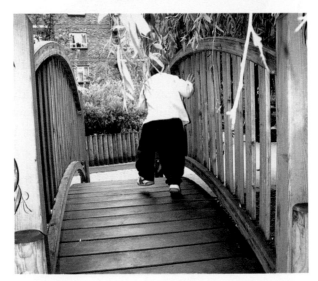

Photo 84

exactly what we are trying to create until we have created it. This is as true for creative adults as it is for children. When we look at how scientists and artists create, we see that the processes which lead to creative products are necessarily fluid and, like play, need to remain in a state of flow and not be set in concrete when they only half-exist at that stage of creativity.

VARIATIONS ON A THEME

Exploring the bridge in the garden leads the boy in the photographs (82–84) to three different ways of interacting with it:

1. he runs from one side to the other, and repeats this over and over again;
2. he then begins crossing the bridge but looking through each gap between the wooden railings as he goes;
3. he then crouches, peeping round the corner of first one end of the bridge and then the other, in a peek-a-boo way.

Finding out and experimenting with doing the same thing in different ways is an aspect of creative processes.

Will the result always be the same?

In the next set of photographs he is using a different strategy. He keeps jumping in the puddle, and is very interested to see if he always gets a splash. It is as if he is asking himself the question, 'Does jumping always cause a splash?' This time he does not vary what he does he wants to check that the same action always brings the same result.

Photo 85

Photo 86

TWO STRATEGIES FOR EXPLORING AND DEVELOPING CREATIVE IDEAS
☐ Variation on a theme
☐ Keep doing the same thing

Varying a theme, and repeating the same thing over and over again, are aspects of schemas. This little boy probably has a trajectory schema (Athey, 1990). A schema is a pattern of behaviour which can be repeated, generalised and used in different situations. He consistently uses lines (trajectories), going back and forth across the bridge in different ways (horizontal trajectories), but also jumping in a line up and down (vertical trajectories) as well as going from side to side towards, into and away from the puddle.

In the last chapter, we shall see that the composer J.S. Bach used one theme and musical key and varied this in eighteen fugues grouped together in a book called *The Art of the Fugue*.

Being offered a wide range of materials through which to develop and express creative ideas

In an earlier chapter it was suggested that it is important to set out water-play clothes on the trolley for children to see immediately on entering the garden. The boy concentrating on how water behaves when you apply a force to it is doing physics (learning about forces). He is the force! He is also taking responsibility for himself by putting on the waterproof trousers and the Wellington boots (photographs 85–86).

When he arrives in the morning the boy in the next photographs (87–89) chooses to spend some time at the water tray. His pattern of repeating behaviour is a different cluster of schemas. He puts water into various containers. He does this by transporting the water from the water tray into the container using the jug, with its lip, thus making it easy to pour the water into the receiving container.

He also uses his fascination with putting liquids into a container in a real-life situation when he helps himself to a drink at the outside drinks table. We can also see that he has brought with him a ball of string which he has put in a container, with the scissors on top. The adult he spends time with when he is in the nursery has allowed him

Photo 87

Photo 88

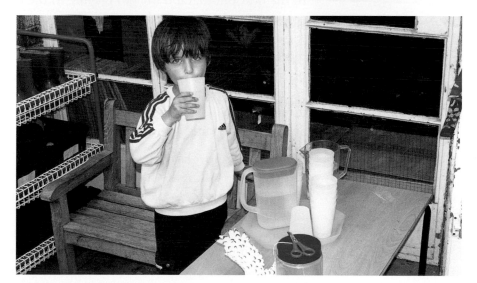

Photo 89

99

to take these from the indoor workshop area, because when he moves from one area of interest to the next, he seems to need to transport something with him. These items can easily be put back later, so that the workshop is not left unequipped. The adult has decided that it is more important that his concentration is not broken as he experiences containers and transporting water, which will cultivate his creative thinking.

Once again we find variations on a theme (containing and transporting in the water tray and pouring a drink) and repeatedly doing the same thing over and over again in different and varied situations and with different materials.

Because he has a wide range of material provision to select from, he was able to find satisfying ways of developing skills and techniques that equip him to develop creative thoughts.

Organising a learning environment which provokes, in many ways, the need to learn skills and techniques useful for lifelong creativity

In the next photograph the girl playing in the home corner is arranging crockery on the tray. She keeps arranging and rearranging the cutlery in the cups she has carefully placed in a line. This is her idea. She also repeats and varies the arrangement. She is using a trajectory schema, placing the cups in horizontal lines and enjoying the linear shape of the cutlery, standing them as vertical trajectories in the cups. She is also using the schema of containing and 'inside/outside' (putting things in and out of the cups, which are containers).

She is very involved in what she is doing, as is the boy both on the bridge and splashing in the puddle, or the boy containing and transporting water. As they select from the experiences they are offered, the children begin to have ideas, some of which show the hallmarks of being creative ideas. The important thing is that the children are given opportunities to make choices and decisions, and they are given sustained periods of time in which to develop their ideas.

Photo 90

The children are not having world-shaking creative thoughts but they are nevertheless having creative ideas as they try things out, rearrange what they know and expect, and explore consistencies and variations. Everyday creativity is as exciting for the person involved as world-shaking creativity is for the world! Because the environment provokes learning and cultivates it, the children are encouraged in their creativity. This is hugely because of the way the adults work with the children. It is also because of the way the experiences and material provision are organised, presented and used with the children.

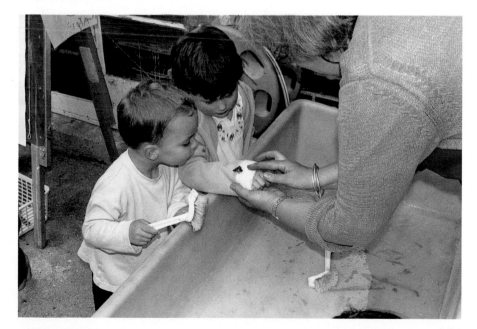

Photo 91

101

However, although this is a well-thought-through learning environment, both indoors and outdoors, it is of fundamental importance to remember to 'seize the moment' when working with children. Things happen quite unexpectedly, spontaneously and in completely unplanned ways. When a moth lands on a child's jacket in the garden, this is a golden opportunity to stop, look, wonder and discuss. Adults might, when it is over and the moth has flown away, and the moment has passed, go to find a book about moths in the bookcase. This could then be looked at later with the children involved, or shown to the group when reporting exciting things that happened that day. This is why a good book resource is essential to a good learning environment. Spontaneous, unplanned events often form the beginning of a creative idea in a child (photograph 91).

Being given the time and personal space, as well as the discussions and respectful help where needed

Children appreciate adults who take the time and make the effort to give them their full attention. Adults working with children will sometimes say that they can't give children individual attention because it is not fair on the other children. This is a misunderstanding of the principles of the equalities. Providing adults keep records and note the kind of support they give every child, then, in a well organised learning environment, every child should receive the adult help and support they need. Not all children are the same. Some need more personal space than others. Some chat with their friends at a very high level of discussion. Others are adult-focused, and anxious when left or when with other children.

It is important to tune into each child's needs, and regular observation of each child, which is then analysed and acted upon, working closely with the parent(s) or carer, helps us to cultivate the creativity and learning of each individual child.

Another reason why adults do not give children individual attention is because they say there is too much going on to free themselves to do this. They argue that they need to supervise children, work with a group, organise activities. This usually means that adults are busying themselves with management of the environment, sweeping up, tidying, 'doing an activity'. Activities take all an adult's attention, when it should be individual children who are given the attention of that adult.

Offering learning experiences, rather than 'doing activities' with children

It is better to think of offering children learning experiences and opportunities, rather than doing activities with them as if children were objects on a conveyor belt. So often we see mass-produced identical butterflies, boats, lambs, Father Christmases etc. made of screwed up tissue paper, filling in an outline, or daffodils made out of cardboard cylinders, cut in the same way on each child's model, to represent the petals. The list is endless. Adults have the idea and the children carry it out under their supervision. The children might be allowed to choose a colour (but not if it is a daffodil, which has to be yellow). The tiny choice the child might be allowed is usually referred to as the child 'personalising' the model. This sort of activity is often misnamed creative. In fact, it could not have less to do with creativity.

It can also be problematic when adults who are themselves creative impose their ideas on children in ways which lack understanding of or respect for children's developing creativity. Sometimes visiting artists, musicians and dancers undertake projects in settings. There is a tendency to have a theme, such as animals, and to invite children to draw an animal, and then make it into a sculpture or relief to be stuck on the wall. This is drawing to order. It would be a remarkable co-incidence if the child decided to draw an animal at exactly the time the artist had requested the child to do so.

This is not the child's idea. It is the adult's idea. This again has nothing to do with the child developing creativity out of their own experience. Neither has the child hatched the idea out and made it into a sculpture or wall relief. The adult has in effect used the child's drawing and turned it into their own agenda.

In this kind of adult-led activity, the child's own creative ideas are not developed. Instead, there is a very public celebration of the adult's ideas, presented as if they are the child's ideas. This undermines the creative ideas that are in the child at the time, and it also has implications for the child's future development. It does not cultivate the child's creativity. It shows no interest in the child's ideas. It only encourages children to participate in the adult's creative agenda. It misleads adults into thinking they are encouraging creativity in children.

Adults who join the play with sensitivity

Something that has a powerful influence on children's creativity is what happens when an adult sits and joins the play as it flows along. In the next photographs (92–93) the adult:

* joins the child;
* tunes in by skilled participative observation;
* finds the child's creative idea;
* helps the child to develop it;
* avoids imposing their ideas and so taking over the child's idea;
* enjoys seeing the child's idea come to fruition in the creation of a story.

We can see what this looks like in practice, in the photographs. The boy has in mind a creative idea which involves making intersections in roads, with cars and lorries using them. Around the outside of the sandpit he puts animals. The adult tunes into his creative idea. She begins to see that he is becoming frustrated because the road keeps collapsing in the centre. She comments on this. She helps him to put a hollow block under the point of intersection, so that it no longer sags. He is pleased, and this enables him to continue developing his creative storying with the cars and lorries on the road. She becomes an interested listener.

Photo 92

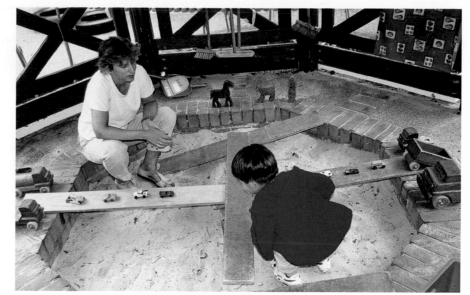

<u>Photo 93</u>

Being helped in the way that is needed at the time

The little girl in the next set of photographs (94–97) is not forced into premature talk about what she will make. After all, she might not 'make' anything. She might simply try out a few creative ideas and there might not be a 'creation' intended to remain. This is why children often show no interest in what they have made. The creative process was the thing. It was never regarded as a creative product by the child.

In the first photograph, we see her choosing which materials she would like to use. She is supported in doing this by the adult. Then she has to decide how to get the nail into the wood. The adult helps her to negotiate a turn at the woodwork bench. This is needed because only two children at a time are allowed here. If she had to do this on her own, it is very likely that she would lose her idea and it would evaporate. As it is, she is helped to bang in the nail. She then uses the glue as paint to cover the nail and the top.

Adults have to make decisions on the spot as they support creativity in action. Should she be allowed to paint with glue? Should she be directed to the paint area? This little girl is not a sufficiently experienced creator to keep hold of her ideas and juggle them with being in the workshop to choose her materials, being at the woodwork area to bang in the nail and then going to the paint area to paint her model white.

105

Photo 94

Photo 95

Photo 96

Photo 97

Her ideas would not be held in her head; they would go. It is best if, although glue is not paint, she is allowed to use the glue as if it were paint on this occasion. The adult might say, 'It looks like paint, doesn't it?', indicating that paint might be good, perhaps next time. It means that not only has she sustained her creative ideas (the process of creativity) but she has managed, with adult support, to bring her idea to fruition (creative product).

The right help in the right way at the right time – skilful adults

The help needed at the woodwork bench is of a different kind from the help needed as a child becomes a dance maker (Davies, 2003: 158). As we saw in an earlier chapter, it is often difficult to distinguish between making and performing dances, especially for young children, 'whose dance is dancing and dancing is the dance'.

Mollie Davies points out that dance creativity in young children 'needs to take place within a broad framework which can be adapted as situations demand'. As adults helping children to create dances of their own, we need to address some questions she raises.

❋ What are the structuring devices for making a dance?
❋ Do they facilitate or restrict the children?
❋ How should we use the structuring devices with a particular child?
❋ Should we use structuring devices at all with young children?

She points out that the first dances young children make tend to be full of contrast: 'at one time gentle and calm, at another fierce and stormy, for example, as it sweeps through the space, makes a bid for the sky and literally collides with the earth'.

Because, as she points out, three- and four-year-olds typically move from one thing to another as they dance, they allow the 'different threads of their dancing to emerge and intertwine'. There is no point or benefit in offering structuring devices to children too early, as they need plenty of time for what Mollie Davies calls 'exploratory dance-play', as we saw in the photographs in an earlier chapter of the two girls dancing in their ballet outfits (photographs 10–13).

However, as Sybil Marshall (1963) says, we need to know enough about the subject to know and understand what the children need to know about making a dance. Mollie Davies says we need to introduce them in the right way at the right time to what she calls dance 'architecture'. This is what Margaret Donaldson emphasised at the beginning of this chapter. Children need our help in learning the culture, whether it is dance, music, mathematics, science, the visual arts, literature or drama. We need to encourage their ingenuity and creativity, giving them the 'basics' in the way Langer (1997) suggests, by helping them to make the basics fit them as individuals, rather than requiring them to fit the cultural norms, boringly and in a commonplace way.

Helping children to be creative learners in the visual arts

John Matthews (2003) points out that self-initiated and self-directed learning in every area is important for babies, toddlers and young children. However, he also stresses the key role of adults in cultivating the creativity of children. He focuses on the way this develops in the visual arts. He uses the metaphor of a developmental landscape with:

many crossroads at which children must choose a direction. Although children sometimes appear to get stuck in apparent impasses, these hold-ups need not be permanent. (Matthews, 2003: 196)

If we observe the children, using our knowledge of how children develop, and alongside this keep learning about the visual arts, we will find that children show us in their 'action, play and media use'

(Matthews, 2003: 196) as well as in words or signs, what they are interested in. We can then give them what they need in ways which help them through an impasse.

Strategies (arising from the work of John Matthews (2003: 200) with children in the UK and in Singapore) which help children through an impasse are:

HELPING CHILDREN THROUGH AN IMPASSE IN CREATIVE LEARNING

☐ When children are frustrated, help them by encouraging them to search the environment for an image or example they want

☐ They might find a photograph, or image of another artist, helpful to look at to see how three dimensions can be translated into two dimensions

☐ Looking at how someone else has done something and using it in your own drawing or painting is not 'copy painting' if it helps you to carry out your idea

☐ Help children to use people who are more experienced than them to show examples of how something can be technically drawn or joined to make a model. Teaching a skill when it is needed is very helpful to children as they develop their creativity

☐ Be genuinely interested in what the children have drawn, painted or made. They are then likely to want to discuss the techniques and content more readily than if you focus only on what interests you

☐ When children share their drawings, paintings and models with you, they are not wanting you to offer a critique ('Where are the teeth?'). They want you to say which bits are interesting ('I like the way you have shaded there. What were you thinking?')

☐ Don't draw or paint for children. Draw for yourself, at your own level, and join in when they draw, so that they see adults drawing and painting as part of everyday living. Talk about the techniques and technical problems as you go

☐ Make sure that showing them you as a sketcher, painter, sculptor is only a small part in a larger approach of your interest in their creativity in the visual arts

Each of these bullets has been related to the visual arts, but they could just as well be used to help children cultivate their creative learning in the humanities, sciences or other arts (dance, music, drama, literature).

Help with making dances, in the right way, at the right time

Because transition from one idea to the next is an important aspect of making a dance, Mollie Davies (2003: 159) suggests that we can be very helpful if we give children experience of opposites, such as 'quick and slow'. Just commenting, 'I noticed you went quick and then very slow' is often enough to bring awareness to the child, and then they can repeat the dance they have made (choreographed) again and again, for family and friends.

Giving children the technical know-how

Every subject has its technical know-how. Sybil Marshall, headteacher of a rural primary school, was an English literature specialist, and gave her children the structural devices needed to write creatively. In order to be able to offer children technical know-how in a variety of subjects, practitioners working with young children need to be as highly educated and well trained as possible, and to see themselves on a learning journey.

Just as poetry needs words and sculpture requires substances like clay or wood, so dance composition needs movement. As children become more and more familiar with the language of dance – the material of movement – they slowly begin to differentiate between the process and the product. Unless they achieve familiarity with a wide range of movement expression, creativity cannot effectively take place. Instead, children will be seen to produce the same movements and movement patterns time and time again. (Davies, 2003: 161)

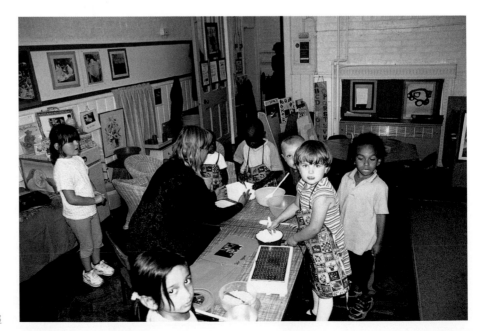

Photo 98

110

We keep coming back to the importance of the adult role in cultivating creativity in young children.

Photo 99
Helping children to develop
technical know-how

THE ADULT ROLE IN HELPING CHILDREN TO BE CREATIVE LEARNERS

☐ Give children wide-ranging, broad, rich experiences which give them choice, opportunities to experiment and find out how materials function

☐ Be interested in what the child is interested in, and don't try to make them change to what you are interested in

☐ Give them sensitive help to follow through their interest by giving them what they need in order to do this

☐ Be a good observer, and study both child development and subjects (dance, science etc.) so that you develop the technical know-how of the subject and also spot the right moment to offer structural devices to the child

☐ When you teach, directly, a skill or technique, don't expect that 'one size fits all'. Remember that you need to help the child make a basic technique fit them as an individual. They need to use the basics (the tennis stroke, the handwriting techniques, woodwork, dance, making a story), to suit them as a unique person

☐ As you help them, give them the techniques and structural devices which will help them to think and be aware of their own learning

CHAPTER 9
CREATIONS

The focus of this book is on cultivating creativity. Creativity has these aspects:

❋ emergent beginnings;
❋ the process of developing a creative thought or idea (being creative);
❋ the product which emerges (being a creator).

It is not possible to have a creative product without it being the result of the creative processes that led to it.

It is possible to develop creative ideas and thoughts which do not emerge and become creative products.

We need to understand the different needs of children as they are involved in the different aspects of creativity. We need to offer the right help at the right time in the right way if we are to cultivate their creativity. We need to give them the opportunities and time to explore, select and meander and find ideas which they may not consciously know they have. We need to structure the environment so that it is conducive to the cultivation of creativity.

Not knowing in advance – an important part of creative processes

In the photographs (100–102) we can see Rosalind finding her way about the workshop area, sifting through materials, without a clear focus but experiencing the materials and getting to know what she wants to do. Although she doesn't seem to react to the boy joining her at the table, and he doesn't seem to interact with her, they probably enjoy each other's companionship. It is a fact that children often avoid or don't stay long at an area if they are alone using it.

Photo 100

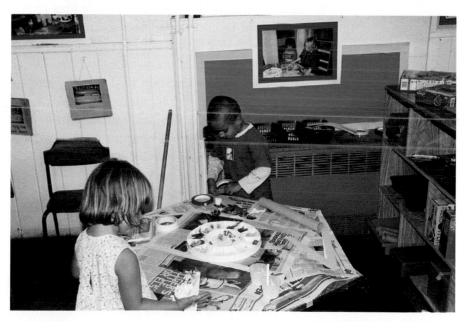

Photo 101

Rosalind (and the boy) begin to develop their thoughts in creative ways. We followed the boy's progression from creative idea being processed into a creative product (the wristwatch) in an earlier chapter.

Photo 102

Here we see Rosalind gathering her thoughts and selecting yellow strips which she sticks onto card. Then she chooses some dried flowers and glues them onto the strip. She seems pleased with this and decides to make a second strip.

This has many connections with Mollie Davies's (Davies, 2003) advice that children move from one idea to another and can gradually be helped to understand a structural device in making a dance if they see how to link one dance idea to another through the structural device of 'transitions'. In this case Rosalind makes a repeated pattern of decorated yellow strips on card, which form stripes. She is unaware of this. She is joined by an adult (the headteacher) who observes before saying anything. She tunes into Rosalind's interest. Because it is not helpful to children to introduce what Mollie Davies calls 'structural devices' too soon or too early, the adult waits to see if it is timely to mention that the second strip is going to look like the first one, and makes a link with the first so that the two together become a striped pattern.

When Rosalind has placed the second strip, and it definitely has become a striped pattern, the headteacher says, 'I like the way the two strips together make a stripe pattern. Very effective'.

As is typical in this sort of situation, Rosalind simply looks at what she has created, and then quickly picks it up and puts it on the display table to dry. The focus of that moment is often an indicator to the skilled and sensitive observer that the child was interested and has become aware of what she has done.

Having creative intentions

Piaget would say Rosalind had an intention she could not articulate in words, and appreciated the adult recognising this.

Bruner would argue that the adult has tuned into the child's incipient intention by talking 'as if' that is what the child had in mind.

Vygotsky would say that Rosalind made this pattern entirely by accident, and it was only because the adult commented on it that she became aware of it. (Vila, 1996).

The development of **intention** is important but, where creativity is concerned, it is often best left as a very flexible thing. This means that children should not be expected to put their intentions into words in advance of what they make or as they are developing an idea. The intention really just needs to be a rough line of a general direction, so that the child can be the one who forms the idea, and the adult doesn't snatch a half-forming idea from them and turn it into their own adult creation. When intention changes from being the child's developing and still-forming creative idea to being the adult's fully-formed idea, creativity in the child is destroyed rather than cultivated.

This was something that emerged when adults worked with children in the Froebel Blockplay Research Project (Gura, 1992: 23) at the Froebel Institute in the 1990s.

THE TEACHERS, PARENTS AND NURSERY NURSES FOUND THAT:
- ☐ problems arise when children are asked to verbalise in advance of action;
- ☐ lack of pressure for the child to speak is important;
- ☐ language without action decontextualises situations;
- ☐ formal advance planning constrains the imagination and discourages flexible thinking;
- ☐ other strategies from the adult may help children to think more effectively in advance about what to do.

A three-year-old girl found a caterpillar in the garden. She arrived next day with a toy caterpillar and decided to make one out of blocks. Then she chose to draw the block model of her toy caterpillar. She found she had added an extra leg on one side. The next day she reconstructed her block model, using the sketch to guide her. She remembered to deduct the extra leg! (Gura, 1992: 23)

We can see from this example that helpful adults have cultivated her creative intentions in ways which are right for her, and with very good

115

results. She has been able to think creatively over time and to make a product which can be reconstructed to look exactly the same again and again.

Sometimes we have a clear idea which restricts our creativity

Often, however, children at about the age of four years become very fascinated by making functional creations. The boys in the photograph below want to use the swords they have made. Note the 'on alert for danger' body language of the adult in the photograph!

Photo 103

The boy in the photographs (104, 105) has been part of the group for nearly two years. He knows his way around the materials and particularly enjoys the woodwork area. He decides to make an aeroplane, and carries out this very clear plan. He then paints it. But is he being creative? Probably not. He has developed a technique for making aeroplanes, so that he can repeat the formula over and over again. We are back to 'structural devices' again (Davies, 2003). It will be important that he varies and innovates around his model aeroplane designs or he will not be a creative learner. The time is now right for him to learn more about the aerodynamics of flight. This is where staff need to learn too. Just as in dance children need to learn the structural devices of how to transition and link one dance idea to

Photo 104

Photo 105

the next, so in engineering and science they need to know about wing and body shapes which allow lift-off. The boy depends on adults to help him in this.

Of course, we do need to be careful because sometimes children are happy if their creation is purely an image that suggests a likeness to something. They don't want it to be functional. The model 'suggests' aeroplane, and that is enough.

Creative process is about creating resources and ideas to be used later

Children often seem to show no interest in keeping the paintings, drawings or models that they make. This is because they are part of the creative process, rather than coming to fruition as a product. Finger painting experiences are not usually about creative products. They give children the opportunity to discover, experience, meander, drift, identify thoughts and ideas, and see how they form. This kind of experience is not about making a creative product.

The same is true of play scenarios. They are not meant to be captured and pinned down into a creative product. They become a reservoir of experiences to be called on for storytelling, poetry making, in literature and drama.

The child who spends hours at the woodwork bench trying things out, varying how they do things, using different materials and tools, is making a future store to be drawn upon. It is a bit like squirrels storing nuts and forgetting where they bury them, then finding them later when they are needed. We sometimes say that children are busy doing nothing. The nothing is crucial as part of creative learning. The girl in the photographs (106, 107, 108) is identifying ideas, selecting, experimenting, varying an action or

Photo 106

Photo 107

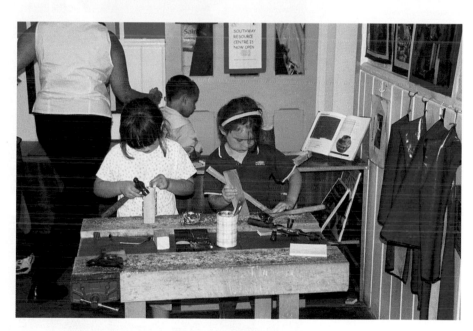

Photo 108

material, gathering ideas, and has the kind of concentration that goes with deep thinking. This kind of creative learning is often discouraged by adults who don't understand the kind of learning that does not look 'purposeful'. This girl's needs are entirely different from the boy who made the aeroplane. Staff have identified that he now needs some direct teaching on aerodynamics. She is like Rosalind, and needs to meander and find her direction before she knows where she wants to go.

Creative ideas grab children as they develop their play scenarios

We can see an idea grab the girl in the photographs and how, when that happens, she has creative ideas she can follow, even if she is not aware they are happening to her. Later in the day she goes into the home corner and pretends to talk on the telephone. She wants her baby to hear what the pretend person on the other end of the phone is saying, so she holds the phone near to the baby's ear. She pretends the baby wants to say something, so she holds the telephone so that the baby can speak.

Photo 109

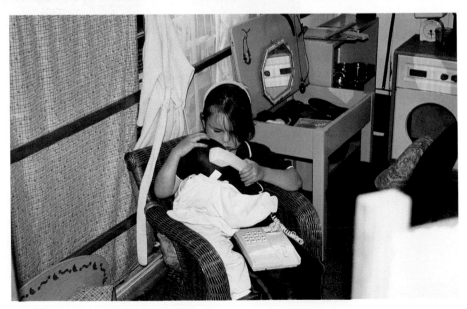

Photo 110

She is being creative, but play of this kind is 'free-flow play' (Bruce, 1991, 2001). It fades when the play fades, and is not meant to be kept. Play is about process and not about keeping products.

We can see this kind of play scenario developing in the next photograph. The boy is engaged in solitary play, talking to himself with the small world train set. This is not a story to keep and turn into a creative product. He needs to flow.

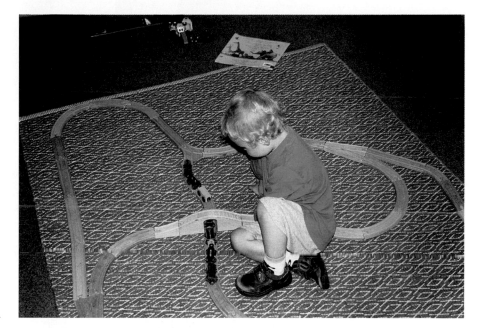

Photo 111

The boy is making a play scenario around the train tracks, but children let stories flow and bubble out using a huge range of media if given the opportunity. He has selected the train track. Children who have only a narrow range of choice (or no choice at all if they are required to fulfill adult-led activities all day) cannot develop their creative ideas using the medium they are most comfortable in. After all, some of us love to dance. Some of us love to paint. Some of us love to make mathematical thoughts and solutions. We all have our preferred media and, if we are allowed to use our strengths, we can learn more deeply and be more creative (flexible and mobile in our thoughts).

Some children love to make drawings to enable their ideas to flow, but when they do, they are unlikely to be bothered about keeping the drawing or seeing it displayed. It is important to ask children if they want a drawing or painting displayed before putting it on a wall. It might have been part of the creative process and not thought of as a definite creation.

Photo 112

In the photograph we can see two drawings which children have wanted to display and are finished creations. The children have pinned them up as if to signal, 'This is a finished creation'.

Dens as creations

Another example of a finished creation is Tom's 'A' house, which he made in the garden when he was seven years old. Sometimes we can see glimmerings of earlier creative influences on a creation. We keep saying throughout this book that, more often than not, we can't tell how a creative idea began. The phase of gradually identifying an idea and gathering thoughts around it usually remains hidden to us. But here we can see that Tom, from the age of about three years, has been using a woodwork bench. He has learnt to join pieces of wood with a hammer and to use a vice. He has been making criss-cross aeroplane configurations since then.

Recently at school the teacher took the children for a mathematical walk as part of a project on triangles and other shapes. She showed the children how triangles are used to strengthen buildings.

A little while after the project, Tom was playing in the garden with a friend and they wanted to build a den. As Lili Nielsen (1992) says, all over the world children build dens as part of their play; Tom and his friend Ben were typical in this. As the day went on, they used their knowledge of triangles and, with a hammer, nails and wood, made an

'A' house, as they called it. They wanted to sleep on the platform, hanging blankets over the apex to make a tent-like construction. They were allowed to do so, and Tom's mother slept nearby in the garden so that they could be safe.

Here we can see the creative learning (process) and how it led to a creation (the 'A' house).

* **Prepare** – unconsciously identifying a vague thought that lingers.
* **Simmer** – gathering thoughts around it, without realising this.
* **Illuminate** – being obviously interested in it, and becoming aware of this.
* **Hatching** – trying to make it more formed and tangible.
* **Hatched** – a creation emerges.

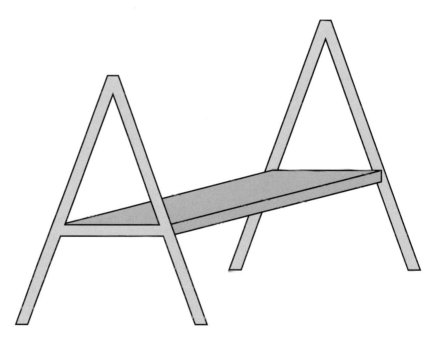

The 'A' house

A completely different example would be Hannah (7 years old) and her friend Anna (6 years old), who made a café. They spent days setting up everything they would need. They begged plastic cutlery from adults, borrowed crockery, made a cash register, invoices, cheque books, and cooked biscuits. They made fresh orange juice, using a recipe. They both attended the cookery club every Wednesday afternoon during school time. They made menus and table cloths from old sheets which they were allowed to decorate using felt pens. They made waitress hats out of folded paper. They had learnt all these techniques at one time or another at school. They were also avid watchers of the BBC television programme for children, *Blue Peter*.

For several days they were involved in 'free-flow play' (Bruce, 1991, 2001), using dolls and various friends to develop the play scenario. John Matthews notes the importance of children having opportunities to flow across several days in their play, especially at this age.

The play scenario turned into a creation when they asked if they could invite neighbours to 'really have tea' in their café, and if they could raise funds for the *Blue Peter* Appeal. They did both, so the 'free-flow play' became a creation which was pinned down and took a definite lasting shape. This was now a café, rather than children playing cafés. They moved from being creative to being creators.

Play scenarios are a powerful resource of ideas for later use

Children, typically from about four years of age, may be happy to tell their play scenarios to an adult, as Vivian Gussin Paley has experienced. They may be happy to dictate them for the adult to scribe and to act them out with friends later at circle time. This is by no means always the case, and Gussin Paley works with great sensitivity with the children on this. Children can go to a specially designated table and dictate their story if they wish, but are under no pressure to do so.

Boys narrate superhero adventures filled with dangerous monsters, while girls place sisters and brothers, mothers and fathers in relatively safe roles. If lost, they are quickly found, if harmed they are healed or replaced. Boys tell of animals who kill or are killed; girls seldom involve animals in violence. A bear or lion encountered in the forest is likely to lead a girl home and will not be shot and eaten for supper. (Gussin Paley, 1981: 204)

In this way, children begin to see how play scenario ideas can be used to create stories which become written down, to become dramas that can be performed again and again.

This is entirely different from the adult artist taking children to see an art exhibition, deciding on a theme of, say, animals, asking each child to draw one, and then using the child's design to make a group wall relief. From start to finish this is the adult's idea and the children are simply participating in the adult's creation.

It is when adults try to formalize creativity that they reduce it as it emerges. Children will draw and paint with great enthusiasm if they are encouraged to have ideas of their own. When adults underestimate or dismiss their ability to do this they stamp out 'any chance of children doing anything original', as Isadora Duncan put it at the beginning of this book.

One of Matthew's first words was 'digger'. He was fascinated by diggers as a toddler and would gaze at diggers he saw at road works. His favourite toy was a digger. It is hardly surprising that one of his first major drawings was of a digger, when he was four years old. It was drawn on scrap paper. He gave it to his grandparents, because he was at their house when he drew it. It was a creation, but it emerged out of the processes of his creative learning.

Matthew's digger

Kit (four years old) also enjoyed drawing at his grandparents' house. His grandfather wrote on the back of one of his drawings:

Having drawn the black parts Kit kept on about something 'sticking out'. Only when he drew the blue water and the diver did we realize that he meant the 'Mary Rose'.

Mary Rose
('ship sticking out')

Diver

Kit's drawing of the
Mary Rose Tudor ship

He had watched a programme on television with his grandparents about the lifting of the Tudor ship the 'Mary Rose'. A few days later he visited them again. They had left a newspaper cutting about this event on a coffee table. He must have noticed this, and he used the idea in his spontaneous drawing on a piece of scrap paper.

For every time we realise the creative thinking that a child is involved in, there are probably many more that we never come to know about.

A typical kind of creation that passes unobserved except to a highly skilled observer can be seen in photograph 113, of the boy and girl loading the trolley in the garden. Between them they make a handle so that they can pull the trolley from the front with the handle already provided, or from the back with their own created handle. This meant they could have more flexibility in the direction they pulled the trolley.

Photo 113

The example of the pulley experience is another of these situations (see photographs 114 to 122). Again there is an adult who is sensitive and quietly protects the children's space and opportunity to develop their creative thinking. Although the trolley experience resulted in a creation – the second handle – in the pulley experience the creativity is in the process. There is no creation.

The boy is in a transition from one thing to finding what attracts him next. Learning to select and finding what interests us is central to being an effective learner in the long term. Children who do not learn to do this lack focus and concentration, and are passive because they have to be introduced to activities by adults all the time.

Photo 114

The boy is attracted to the sand but hesitates to go into the area. The adult encourages him by saying, 'That's good. You're going to play with the sand are you?' He nods and goes in. He uses his previous experience and knowledge and understanding of how the pulley works, and all goes well

Photos 115 and 116

Photos 117 and 118

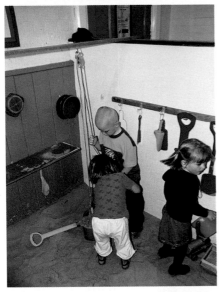

until he finds that the bucket of sand is too heavy for him to lift. As so often happens, at the moment of 'impasse', as John Matthews calls it, a girl sees the problem and joins him. I do not know if this is a gender issue but, during my thirty years of experience, time and again this seems to happen: girls seem to be good at noticing problems out of the corner of their eye and trying to help out without taking over.

Between them, the two children manage to lift the bucket of sand with the pulley. The girl has varied the technique, which is a creative response, so that two people pull the rope and not one. This is the sort of creativity Ellen Langer emphasises as important in her example of the basic tennis strokes. Unless people can use them with creative flexibility and variation to fit the people and situation, they will not be effective learners.

Photos 119 to 122

After his efforts with the pulley, the boy leaves the sand area. He sees a friend playing with the wooden unit blocks and the lorries (photograph 123). He joins him, using a classic access strategy. Corsaro (1979) calls this a 'side-by-side' strategy. The boy does the same as his friend, making an enclosure and placing a lorry in it. The friend watches, and accepts his contribution to the play (photographs 124 and 125).

This is very fascinating to observe. The boy has noticed that his friend is making enclosures and putting lorries inside the enclosure. By imitating this, he is signalling to his friend that he has recognised his creation, and that it is a pattern that can be repeated again and again so that the block construction keeps expanding. His friend feels that his creation is valued and recognised. They repeat the creation (enclosure with lorry inside it) again and again, taking it in turns to do so.

We sometimes think that only adults appreciate the creativity of children. We can see in this example that children appreciate each other's creativity, but often do not, perhaps cannot, express this in words. Words or signs are good for some kinds of communication, but not for every situation. Here, no words are needed.

Diane Dunkin and Pamela Hanna give some guidance on the different kinds of responsive and reciprocal interactions adults can make with children. As we can see, children also use these strategies when they communicate well with each other:

When we follow the child's lead, in their action or words, we are supporting them in a positive way to share and develop their own thinking, instead of directing, telling or showing them what to think or do. When we demonstrate positive regard for the child and respect for their ideas and feelings, we foster their sense of identity – an important factor in self-confidence and self-esteem. (Dunkin and Hanna, 2001: 33)

Photo 123

Photo 124

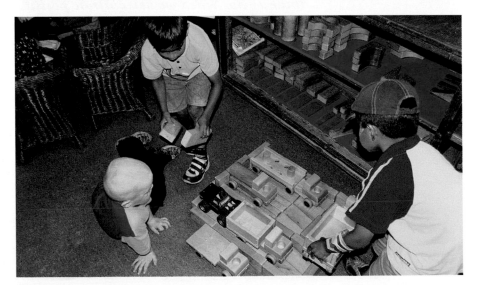

Photo 125

We can tune into someone else's creative idea and appreciate their creation by:
- ☐ doing the same thing and using the person's idea;
- ☐ talking about what is happening;
- ☐ rephrasing what the other person says, and putting it into our own words;
- ☐ making parallel remarks: 'I've made an enclosure just like yours. Now I'm going to put a lorry in it, like you did'.

The volcano

Children love nooks and crannies as well as wide-open spaces in which to run about. Creative ideas often develop in hidden away places off the beaten path. The entrance hall, where an adult greets families on arrival and stays on to chat to children, is a good example of this.

When children know there will be an adult interested in helping them to develop their deepest thoughts, they find their way to that spot with regularity. On this particular morning, two boys decide to make a volcano. They find a cloth, and place scraps of paper on it to represent the lava. The adult, as if by magic, has a book about volcanoes. This is a crucial element in the creative process. Because there is a great emphasis on building a good fiction and non-fiction library, books on every subject can be produced in seconds. Staff know the library they have developed inside out, and distribute the books around the building according to the children's interests and needs.

Photo 126

Photo 127

Photo 128

Girls begin to join the volcano building. There is plenty of discussion about volcanoes along the way. This is another very important point. This really is discussion, rather than the adult telling the children about volcanoes. Children's scientific stories are listened to and built on.

One of the boys thinks that the orange playdough in the main room would be just right for the lava. The adult encourages him to fetch some, suggesting he should tell an adult in the room why he needs it. This is another important aspect of the way adults work with the children. There is a team commitment to cultivating creativity in the children. This means that strict adherence to narrowly followed rules is not the order of the day. Instead there are clear and firm boundaries

Photo 129

which the children help to make, so that the environment is safe and equipment is not damaged. Whether dough can be removed is open to negotiation as situations arise.

The children know that they will need to discuss any changes to the usual boundaries. Once the temporary change in boundary can be seen to be official, and because the orange dough is carefully placed on the volcano, other children begin to bring playdough. We see them imitating and using the 'side-by-side' strategy as they place their 'lava' alongside his to run down the slopes of the volcano.

At the end of the morning, the volcano is left as a creation in the entrance hall for others to appreciate. The intensity and depth of

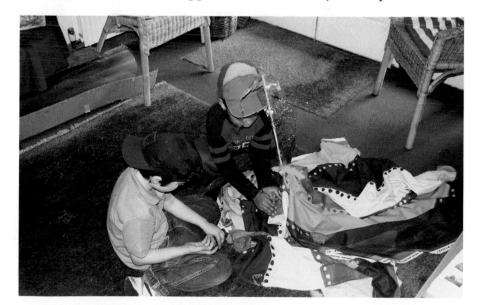

Photo 130

creative thinking that developed (the process) was an important reason why the volcano became a creation (product). We can see that being creative thinkers led the children into becoming creators – of a volcano.

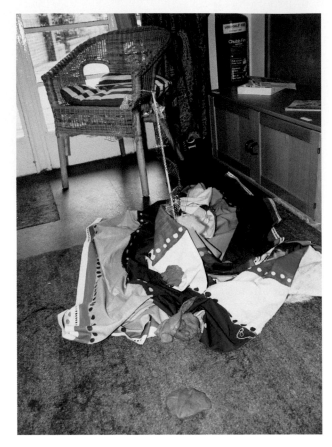

Photo 131

Penny Holland (2003) suggests that adults need to be more sensitive to the needs of boys in their dramatic play scenarios, and to tune into their themes, even when they look as if they are going in directions of weapon play. Vivian Gussin Paley also agrees that boys tackle themes of killing and death in their play scenarios more than girls. The volcano is violent. Children need to explore life and death scenes in their play, and at times will capture these in their creations.

Creations

The creations children make are very personal. They will share them only with those they trust and by whom they feel respected. There is nothing as deeply satisfying as sharing with a child the hatching out of a creative idea and finding that it has become a creation.

CHAPTER 10
EVERYDAY CREATIVITY, SPECIALIST CREATIVITY AND WORLD-SHAKING CREATIVITY

In this book, as we have seen in earlier chapters, the word 'creativity' is used as an umbrella term, with these three aspects under it:

1. spotting the signs of the emergent **beginnings of creativity**;
2. **being a creative learner**;
3. making **creations**.

We have looked at the beginnings of creativity in an earlier chapter, and throughout the book there has been an emphasis on the way that creative learning can be cultivated in young children. Sometimes, but not always, a creation emerges.

Everyday creative learners

For the most part, the creations of young children, whether they are from the visual arts, scientific theories, mathematical patterns and ideas, dances, musical improvisations or the creative way of relating to people and resolving conflicts and fairness issues, are of the everyday kind. This is not peculiar to children. It is the same for the majority of adults too. Cooking a delicious meal, creative in its combination of ingredients, improvised from what is found in the fridge, cupboard and vegetable rack, is a much-appreciated kind of everyday creativity by those who share the meal with the cook.

Creativity in everyday life lifts living to levels of fulfilment, satisfaction, effective, deep and rigorous practical thinking which are in a different league to pedestrian, boring and commonplace living. Creativity makes life worth living, especially when the going is tough. It is linked with resilience and, in extreme cases, with survival. It means that we are using our intelligence to the full, flexibly, adaptively and imaginatively as we problem-solve and generate new thoughts.

Being creative in everyday life is a good way of living. It develops a strong sense of self as a separate, autonomous person, with a sense of agency and control over what we can do to change things for the better. Being a creative learner also gives a sense of belonging and connectedness with others, and the knowledge that it is possible to contribute as well as take in life, and make things better not just for oneself but for others too.

Most of this book is about cultivating everyday creative learning in young children, so that in their daily lives, throughout their lives, they will plan what they eat, cook, how they present their food, plan what they wear, arrange their homes, gardens, leisure interests and work and be creative as they do so. Some of us like to put our main emphasis on our leisure time and work, and not so much on daily shopping and home-making. Others are more focused on creative cooking, DIY, gardening and décor. Different people are creative in different ways – providing their creativity has been cultivated and not constrained or stamped out at an early stage or though lack of use.

EXAMPLES OF CREATIVE APPROACHES TO LIVING

- ☐ Making up a food recipe
- ☐ Choosing your own design for a room (not copying an existing one)
- ☐ Redesigning your own garden, using your own ideas
- ☐ Drawing your own tapestry design and choosing the coloured threads to use
- ☐ Making a cupboard with your own design
- ☐ Making a dress or shirt by combining several paper patterns to fit your ideas of what you want
- ☐ Planning a social gathering and carefully getting people together so that they enjoy it as much as possible
- ☐ Planning a car route to take in scenery and good picnic spots suitable both for grandma, who has a Zimmer frame but loves to be in the countryside, and for a niece who is prone to hay fever
- ☐ Making music and dance together with a large group at a party

---

Specialist creative learners

There are many people who are highly expert in a particular area, who are completely unknown outside their field but who nevertheless are creative learners, finding deep satisfaction in the ideas they develop and bring to creation.

In the photograph (132), we can see a group of girls chatting about what is happening in their play scenario with the doll's house. It is very hard to establish any links between childhood play and later imagination and creativity. Researchers who take a hard line would say there is no evidence to claim that childhood play causes later creativity and imagination.

Photo 132

Looking at the childhood play of creative adults, artists, scientists and those involved in the humanities, gives us some hints. Until recently there seemed to be only an associative link between smoking and cancer; through research, this has been recognised as a causal link. At the moment there are only glimpses of what might be associative links between childhood play and adult creativity.

Brain development and creativity

We are beginning to understand more about how the brain develops (Carter, 1999). Children born into musical families hear music played from the beginning, and from an early age participate in music-making with their family. Studies reveal that these musicians have larger parts of the brain colonised for sound in the area that deals with language. This suggests that the more we use our brains to develop our creativity, the more we can be creative.

Let us return to the doll's house play scenario. The doll's house has been an important tradition in early childhood practice in the UK and other countries for a century or more. We don't know if the children in the photograph will later in their lives use their doll's house play as a resource, but we do know how this kind of play influenced one adult artist, Katie Etheridge.

The visual arts

Katie is an installation artist. Her work is of great interest to those working with young children because it makes powerful links with her childhood experiences. In her work she uses the doll's house, her enjoyment of wearing dressing-up clothes and dancing, and the bones of a horse that she found as a child when on a family holiday in the New Forest. A video is projected onto the back wall of the large doll's house, featuring dancers dressed as the dolls who live in the doll's house. They move from room to room as they dance. The staircase is made out of the spine of the horse's skeleton. Katie says of her installation, which is named *All that Remains*:

Dolls' houses, as miniature worlds created by children that they can control, relate back to the desire to make sense of the world.

Another part of her installation shows a video of a long-forgotten music hall dancer placed in a cabinet, which, she says:

… invites thought on what is the sum of someone's life once they are gone, and how do they live on through the things they leave behind?

She continues:

Collecting and sorting can be a way of trying to create order in a volatile and unpredictable universe. We turn our homes into miniature museums, choosing what to display and what to keep hidden away, inadvertently curating the remnants of our lives. Likewise, memories are ordered and filed by the unconscious mind. Some may lie buried deep and untouched for years. The objects we hold on to are historical artefacts in their own right, but also embody a deeper and entirely personal significance as triggers of memory. But what happens when we die and become relics ourselves? (Etheridge, 2001: 9)

We can see very clearly that her childhood experiences with a very happy family holiday, the loss of a loved person, her play with dolls' houses and her enjoyment of dancing, have all been part of the development of her ideas, which have resulted in a creation – an installation called *All that Remains*.

History

Our creative processes and the creations which emerge as a result revolve around people as well as objects, as we see in this work. The same may be said of Charlotte. She is a historian, studying the Cromwellian period. She takes part in historic re-enactments with a historical society. This involves making a costume that is historically accurate and reconstructing events of battles of that time. She has also constructed, with others, a character for herself, so that the re-enactment has some of the qualities of a drama improvisation. The framework is set by the historic facts, but history is also about people and how they experience events as unique individuals.

As a child, Charlotte spent many hours wearing dressing-up clothes and assuming different characters. Once again, we can see a resonance between her childhood play and her later creativity in the humanities.

Dance choreography

Hannah, on her fifth birthday, was given a cerise tutu. Her choreography changed, particularly as she had been very struck by seeing excerpts from *La Sylphide*. She spent a great deal of time trying to persuade her friend Wally to wear her kilt, like the male lead dancer in *La Sylphide*. She wanted him to lift her. He was not enthusiastic. Over the next few years she was continually frustrated in her desire to choreograph dances for others to perform. She was often clear what she wanted, and could obviously see dances in her head, but getting other children to perform them when they did not know how to dance the steps was a problem.

She found it easier to develop drama improvisations with her friends, and in her middle childhood there were several months when a prolonged play scenario took place in a dress shop, with a complaints department, accounts department and dress-making department, as well as fitting rooms and fashion shows.

It is as if 'a silent refrain from the future' is woven into a child's play, almost waiting for helpful adults to 'pick up the frequency' (Lively, 1993: 7). Adults who do 'pick up the frequency' can make a huge contribution to the future adult's creative development. It is these 'silent refrains from the future', which are fascinating when we observe young children such as Katie with her doll's house, Charlotte with her dressing-up clothes, Tom with his den building, Hannah with her dancing, Matthew with the mechanics of the digger or Kit with the beauty of the Mary Rose.

Hannah as an adult knows enough about the structure of different dance forms to make innovative, creative choreography of her own, blended with her knowledge of literary texts to make a very abstract dance based on Virginia Woolf's book *Moments of Being*. This is a long way from the little girl in the pink tutu, but the beginnings were there.

Resonances between childhood play and adult creativity

It is of course speculative to wonder if there could be any links between the childhood play and the adult creativity in these individuals' areas of specialism. As adults, Katie is an artist, Charlotte has a serious hobby in Cromwellian re-enactments, Tom is studying carpentry, Matthew is a doctor, Kit reads philosophy and poetry in his leisure time, Hannah leads a mixed-media group in dance, drama, film and literary texts. We can ponder what the future creativity will be of Lauren, a newly fledged walker, talker and pretender, putting dolls in and out of the doll's house, and many other children in this book. We can hope it will continue to be cultivated throughout their education as well as at home.

We know that doctors, dancers, writers, musicians, artists, historians, geographers, scientists, mathematicians develop the appropriate skills and technical know-how of their specialisms, but they need to do more than this if they are to be creative in their chosen subject of expertise. In order to go beyond commonplace knowledge of their specialism, they need to be able to use the basics of the subject flexibly. This means they use what they know intelligently and adaptively, and think of new ways of doing things, often because what they know doesn't quite work in a particular situation. We saw this in the example Ellen Langer gave when the basic technique they had been taught for playing tennis was varied and altered by tennis stars so that it would suit them as individuals.

When a doctor makes a diagnosis, it is not enough to know the basics. The basic knowledge has to be actively interpreted and thought about. This is how new medical techniques come about.

Creativity goes beyond the basics

Charlotte can do more than interpret Cromwellian re-enactments. She has, as an adult with an interest in the history of this period, developed a character for her Cromwellian self, complete with costume and artefacts and is part of an imaginary Cromwellian family of characters, improvised with others during each re-enactment. This is a creative way of learning history. Re-enactments of scenes are not a new idea, but Charlotte brings new ideas to this through the character she has created. This is more than everyday creativity, because she has developed great depth of knowledge as she has gathered her ideas about this period of history. This means that she has become a specialist creator.

Scientific creativity

Sometimes we can clearly see how an everyday situation is looked at anew by a creative learner who has developed specialist knowledge. We are going to look at one of several creative contributions made by one scientist, to the study of crystals in chemistry. Here is the story of how this happened.

(A)   (B)

(C)

(D)   (E)

Crystals are part of our everyday lives

Few people realise just how important crystals are, and yet they are part of our everyday lives. We wear them on our wrists or drive about in cars, trains and aeroplanes made of them, or use them to eat with, and many other things. This is because all metal objects are made from crystals, stuck together to form the components of watches, motor vehicles, knives, forks and so on. The reason that we are not aware of this is that they are usually so small that these tiny crystals can only be seen using powerful microscopes.

The crystals we do see in our everyday lives are those such as the sugar we crush in the bottom of a tea cup, or coarse salt we use in cooking. This helps us to see how crystals can be brittle and break up when we crush or grind them.

Why are some things brittle while some are not?

A scientist called Peter Rowland, who is an expert in the behaviour of metal, wanted to look at why we can bend metal wire without it crumbling to pieces, because metal wire is made up of brittle crystals. He decided a good way to do this would be to make models, using spheres to represent the atoms that make up the crystals in the metal wire.

In any crystal, the atoms are arranged in a regular pattern, like the three-dimensional bricks in a wall. To make a model of a crystal that contains enough atoms to be worth studying, he had to put together thousands of spheres in a regular three-dimensional pattern. It was a painstakingly long task.

He developed a creative way of doing this. He poured the spheres into a mathematically designed mould that ensured that they automatically lined up in the same way as would the crystals of a simple metal (like copper).

Photograph A shows a model of this crystal arrangement, (which has since been made into a work of art, because crystal formations are very beautiful). Ping-pong balls have been used to represent the atoms in copper.

The interesting thing was that Peter Rowland found when the model was made in this way it could change form (deform) without the crystal structure breaking up. It wasn't brittle!

Crystal twins

This can be seen in photograph B, where two diagonally opposite corners of the top surface have been pushed towards each other until the mould (and the crystal in it) have been transformed into two. To show this more clearly, figure C shows the mould alone in its transformed state.

* One side is the blue pyramid with its top (apex) pointing to the right.
* One side is the pink pyramid with its tip pointing to the right.

These two pyramids are mirror-images of each other, just as are the patterns of atoms inside them. They are called 'crystal twins'.

Squares, triangles and rotations – transformations!

Before the crystal structure transformed into the twin crystal pyramids, the top layer was a square pattern. It is as if the rotation made the two halves point in different directions and, in so doing, became two triangles!

The rotation came about because the layers of atoms in each half were sliding over each other in parallel directions. The direction was different for the stacks of atoms in the blue and pink pyramids. Figures D and E give some idea of how this happens.

The important thing is that the crystals can bend by the sliding of layers in this way. That is why a copper wire can bend. The crystals of sugar and salt can't bend in this way, so they are brittle and can be crushed and crumbled. Of course, it isn't quite as simple as that but, as we are not expert scientists, this gives us enough understanding to see that the model which metallurgists named, after its discoverer, the 'Rowland Transformation', helps scientists to know how transformations of this kind affect the strength, hardness and general properties of metals.

This is a good example of how something was staring mathematicians in the face for several thousand years before being spotted. It took a metallurgist, puzzling out how a piece of metal wire can bend, to see the structural connection with ancient geometrical constructions such as the pyramid-shaped piles of spherical stone missiles found in prehistoric forts, which are really upside-down versions of photograph A.

In this story of a scientist's journey we have seen how he was involved in the creative processes of:

* preparation
* incubation
* illumination
* hatching

143

which resulted in a creative product: the Rowland Transformation model (1954).

Philip Pullman (2002), the writer, says there are three things he would like people who work with children to invoke, in order to cultivate a child's creativity:

1. **Mystery**
   By mystery, I mean the delicate … trance-like business of letting a story come at you out of the shadows, without pestering it and jabbing questions at it like sticks.

2. **Chance**
   By chance, I mean … experience of other things than educational … unpredictable catching fire that is most memorable.

3. **Silence**
   By silence, I mean the freedom to … wander at will from one interesting thing to another, making no noise, drawn only by delight, and then to settle into the quiet and solitude of your own space and begin the long process of turning all you've gathered into honey.

He ends by saying, 'That would be a National Curriculum worth having'.

In England there are serious concerns about the appropriateness of the Key Stage 1 curriculum which begins for children in the term in which they are five years old. There is often a major discontinuity with the approach and philosophies of the *Birth to Three Matters* Framework (DfES, 2002) and the *Curriculum Guidance for the Foundation Stage* (QCA/DfES, 2000). In other countries of the UK the discontinuity is not so abrupt.

The 'trance-like business' that Philip Pullman describes is rather like the period of preparation that is an important part of developing a creative idea that might be:

* scientific, like Peter Rowland's thoughts about grinding salt when we cook, mixed with vague thoughts about how the Egyptian pyramids were built and the bendiness of copper wire;
* of the humanities, like Nelson Mandela's Council of Reconciliation, which we shall look at next;
* artistic, like the dancer Isadora Duncan, whom we met at the beginning of the book, or the composer J.S. Bach whom we shall meet at the end of the book.

The things that 'unpredictably catch fire' inside our minds and hearts and bodies are like the period of incubation as we develop our ideas, without realising we are doing so, but becoming aware that something exciting is going on inside us.

The way we are 'drawn by delight' about the interest we find in certain things leads to the illumination that comes with the development of a creative idea.

The 'honey' at the end of this process is the hatching out of a creation.

World-shaking creators

People who are world-shaking creators are rare. In this section of the chapter, we shall look at three. They come from different cultures and different historical times.

The humanities

The humanities deal with time, space and reasons for how people behave and structure their lives. The humanities include disciplines such as history, geography and the social sciences (e.g. psychology, anthropology and sociology).

Nelson Mandela, addressing the problem of acknowledging and acting on the way innocent people were tortured, murdered and terrorised during the period of apartheid in South Africa, created the Council of Reconciliation after he was elected President. This was an original idea of enormous implication because, for the first time in the history of that country, there was a spirit of reconciliation instead of a desire to punish through revenge, or through deterring others by public punishment and the humiliation of those who take part in the abuse of human rights. Punishment can be of three kinds:

1. revenge – an eye for an eye and a tooth for a tooth;
2. deterrent – putting people off committing a crime (e.g. a crime against humanity);
3. reform – helping people to admit what they have done, to see why it was wrong, and to do something about their future behaviour because they want to change and not because someone is forcing them to change.

The Nuremberg Trials after the Second World War were in the spirit of revenge and deterrence. The Council of Reconciliation set up by Nelson Mandela was in the spirit of reform.

The sciences

The Polish astronomer Nicolas Copernicus (1473–1543) completed *De Revolutionibus* in 1530. He showed how the Earth rotated on its axis once daily, moving round the Sun once a year. This meant that the Earth was not the centre of the universe. This innovative and original theory changed the way scientists, and now most people, look at the stars and planets. It was called the Copernican Revolution. Because it was dangerous to suggest the Earth was not the centre of the universe, as the Christian Church regarded any threat to its doctrines as heresy to be punished by torture and death, Copernicus did not dare to publish his work and it was not published during his lifetime.

The arts

Interestingly, we cannot really talk about world-shaking creators in the arts, because everyone responds to dance, visual arts, literature and music in a very personal way. That is the whole point about them. That is the whole strength of the arts. Through the arts we can find creators who touch our hearts as well as our minds.

J.S. Bach (1685–1750), during the last year of his life, composed eighteen fugues, published in a book called *The Art of the Fugue*.

❋ He used one theme.
❋ He always wrote in the form of music called a fugue.
❋ He wrote all eighteen fugues in the same key of music.

But it really was an extreme case of variations on a theme! He made the pieces incredibly complex in the way that he varied the number of voices. In the penultimate fugue he inserted the letters of his name, BACH. This is called self-reference, and it has been suggested (Hofstadter, 2000: 86) that he was marking the closure of his life in this way, giving a sense of completion to it. His son, Carl Philipp Emanuel (1750), wrote, 'I have let this final page of Bach's last fugue serve as an epitaph'.

Everyday creativity again

Just as J.S. Bach used variation on a theme and repetition to write his last works of music, so we see young children developing the same strategies. It is as if they are biologically and socio-culturally driven to do so. In an earlier chapter we saw a little boy doing just this in the creative way he used the bridge in the garden (photographs 82–84). In these photographs (135–138) we see Kim-Anh at home, going round and round, time and again, on her scooter. She goes through the living area, dining area, and into the hall, stopping at the front door. Sometimes she ends with a foot on either side of the scooter. Sometimes she ends with a foot on the right side and another on the scooter. Sometimes she ends with both feet on the scooter, and leaps off just in time to avoid crashing into the front door. She is deeply involved and focused in her creative thinking.

Photo 135

Photo 136

Photo 137

Photo 138

> thank you for
> the lovely
> preset love
> from william

It is interesting to find how often children, as J.S. Bach did, use their own name as an important reference point in their creativity. William (seven years) does this when writing a 'thank you' letter to his grandparents. His creativity is not constrained; he feels able to celebrate the gift he has received, and the joy bubbles through in the handwriting. This is not a commonplace, dutiful piece of writing. It would not score high on punctuation, spelling, letter formation or content, but it went to his grandparents' hearts, which is what a 'thank you' letter should do. It held a creative idea, decorating the letters with spirals, which he was able to develop and make into a creation.

> wanst there
> was a
> swalow.
> He flie liet
> to flii High
> and swoop.
>
> The ead d

He showed a different kind of creativity when he tried his first piece of free writing. Once again, this would score low in the English National Curriculum end of Key Stage 1 Standard Assessment Tasks. But the story reflects his love of birds and his fascination with how they fly and how wings work. It shows his assertiveness in marking the end of the story, just to be clear that he doesn't want any adults to suggest he should write more. The story is complete and succinct, and needs no more to be said. It has a visual quality because the letters change size and position in the last sentence as the swallow swoops. It gave him great pleasure to write this story. Again, adults helped him, rather than constraining his creativity, by giving him the personal space to develop his creative idea.

The first seven years are the most effective period in cultivating the creativity of children as lifelong learners

Joanna Glover writes that typically:

Around the age of 6 or 7, children cross a watershed in their musical thinking that brings a new possibility into play in terms of music-making. This is the point at which they become able not just to make, but to think of, musical 'pieces' as such. The realisation comes that the music they create has its own existence, as apart from the activity of making it. The music can be listened to, sung or played by others, captured and kept, and revisited at any time. (Glover, 2000: 55)

She gives a delightful example of a seven-year-old girl saying she had made a 'composement'. However, Glover stresses that whilst children come to understand that a musical composition, a dance they choreograph, a story they write or a mathematical pattern they make can be repeated again and again, it is also important to continue to encourage the other side of creativity, which lies in the continuous and lifelong development of its processes. Joanna Glover therefore values opportunities which give children time and provision for musical improvisations.

This is a serious point, since, as Linda Pound and Chris Harrison (2003: 139–140) point out, 'Most of the singing in schools and nurseries is of songs that have been written by others'.

Starting school – a vulnerable moment for the development of creativity

In most parts of the world, most children do not start their schooling until the age of six or seven years.

Children who have been encouraged to develop deep interests which absorb them and allow them to be separate individuals are also strengthened in their learning to make deep connections and relationships with other people. They put energy into becoming symbol users, with flights of imagination and technical and structural strategies they can bring to bear so that ideas can become creations, when wanted by the child.

In this book we have seen that the emergent, early flickerings of creativity are there in babies and toddlers. If we are determined, creativity can be an inclusive part of human development. If these beginnings are cultivated, they begin to develop into increasing possibilities for being a creative thinker who, from time to time, when the situation is conducive, will make creations that might be of the humanities, artistic or scientific.

For many reasons, it is worth cultivating creativity in babies, toddlers and young children. Young children who have learnt what it is to be creative and to create are beginning to see that they can deepen the enjoyment, fascination and commitment to learning and living when they have found ways in which to put energy into their creative selves.

How to cultivate creativity

✳ Don't believe it is an innate gift or talent, given only to a few. Any child has the possibility to develop creativity.

✳ Don't believe that only 'clever' children can be creative.

✳ Creativity is found in the arts, sciences and the humanities. It is in all areas of human knowledge and learning.

✳ Crafts and creativity are not the same. Be sure to know the difference, and to value each in different ways.

✳ Performing dances, music, etc. is not the same as creating dances and music. Be sure to know the difference.

✳ Children with disabilities can be creative too. Creativity embraces diversity and includes everyone.

✳ Creativity does not mean encouraging revolution and chaos in children.

✳ Children are more able to be creative if they feel loved, valued and that they matter. They need to feel emotionally safe.

✳ Creativity is about knowing yourself, and valuing your personal space.

✳ Creativity requires children to be autonomous enough to have a sense of control over materials and how they use them.

✳ Children often like to be in the company of others they trust when they create.

✳ Creativity brings into existence new ideas, and original ways of doing things.

✳ Creative ideas need to be gathered, and prepared, to incubate then to hatch.

✳ Adults are important in cultivating a child's creativity.

✳ The quality of the learning environment is of central importance indoors and outdoors in encouraging creativity.

✳ Emergent creativity, being creative and actually making a creation are different aspects of cultivating creativity. They help each other along.

✳ The process of creativity is as important as the product.

✳ The creations children make are very personal, and children may not want to share them widely.

✳ Children need the right help at the right time.

✳ Children need to be helped to develop the technical know-how necessary in order to be creative.

✳ Most creativity is of the everyday kind. Some people become specialists in a particular kind of creativity. Some make world-shattering creations that change the world.

✳ The first seven years are a crucial time in cultivating a child's creativity.

Bibliography

Abbott, L. and Moyles, H. (1999) *Early Education Transformed.* Falmer Press: London.

Athey, C. (1990) *Extending Learning: A Parent/Teacher Partnership.* Paul Chapman Publishing: London.

Bartholomew, L. and Bruce, T. (1993) *Getting to Know You: A Guide to Record Keeping in Early Childhood Education and Care.* Paul Chapman Publishing: London.

Bettelheim, (1977) *The Uses of Enchantment.* Vintage Books: New York.

Blakemore, S.J. (2000) Early Years Learning. *Parliamentary Office of Science and Technology Report 140,* pp. 1–12.

Bruce, T. (1991) *Time to Play in Early Childhood Education and Care.* Hodder and Stoughton: London.

Bruce, T. (2001) *Learning Through Play: Babies, Toddlers and the Foundation Years.* Hodder and Stoughton: London.

Bruce, T. and Meggitt, C. (2002) *Child Care and Education, Third Edition.* Hodder and Stoughton: London.

Bruce, T. (2004) *Developing Learning in Early Childhood.* Paul Chapman Publishing: London.

Bunting, J. *Learning through Sustained Imaginative Play at Tachbrook Nursery School.* Centre for Literacy in Primary Education (CLPE) for the City of Westminster.

Burgers, W. and Verbraakt, C.A. (1957) A new approach to the problem of the origin of the cube-texture Rowland Transformation. *Acta Metallurgica*, 1957, Vol. 5, No. 12, pp. 765–767.

Carr, M. (1999) Being a learner: Five dispositions for early childhood. *Early Childhood Practice: The Journal for Multi-Professional Partnerships,* Vol. 1, No. 1, pp. 81–100.

Carter, R. (1998) *Mapping the Mind.* Seven Dials: London.

Christiansen, A. (2002) Play, imagination and communication: Analyses of mobile phone play. *Early Childhood Practice: The Journal for Multi-Professional Partnerships,* Vol. 4 No. 2, pp. 50–61.

Corsaro, W. (1979) 'We're friends, right?' Children's use of access rituals in a nursery school. *Language in society,* Vol. 8, pp. 315–316.

Craft, A. (2002) *Creativity and Early Years Education: A Lifewide Foundation.* Continuum: London & New York.

Damasio, A. (1999) *The Feeling of What Happens: Body and Emotion in the Making of Consciousness.* Heinemann: London.

Davies, M. (2003) *Movement and Dance in Early Childhood.* Paul Chapman Publishing: London.

DfES (2002) *Birth to Three Matters.* Sure Start/DfES.

Dixon, P. (2003) *Weepers: A Collection of Poems Lamenting the Disgraces of the National Curriculum in Primary and Nursery Education.* 30 Cheriton Road, Winchester, Hants.

Donaldson, M. (1992) *Human Minds: An Exploration.* Allen Lane, The Penguin Press: London.

Duffy, B. (1998) *Supporting Creativity and Imagination in the Early Years.* Maidenhead, Philadelphia: Open University Press.

Duncan, I. (1930) *My Life.* Victor Gollancz: London.

Dunkin, D. and Hanna, P. (2001) *Thinking Together: Quality Adult/Child Interactions.* New Zealand Council for Educational Research: Wellington, NZ.

Edmunds, F. (1979) *Rudolf Steiner Education: The Waldorf Schools.* Rudolf Steiner Press: London.

Elkington, J. (2001) *The Chrysalis Economy: How Citizens, CEOs and Corporations can Fuse Values and Value Creation.* Capstone: Oxford.

Etheridge, K. (2001) All that remains: Parts 1 and 2. A mixed media installation. *Early Childhood Practice: The Journal for Multi-Professional Partnerships.* Vol. 3, No. 2, pp. 7–9.

Fabius, C. 1998) *Mehndi: The Art of Henna Body Painting.* Three Rivers Press: New York.

Forbes, R. (2004) *Beginning to Play from Birth to Three.* Open University Press: Maidenhead, Philadelphia.

Glover, J. (2000) *Children Composing 4–14.* Routledge Flamer: London.

Goddard-Blyth, S. (2000) First steps to the most important ABC. *Times Educational Supplement,* 7th January, p.23.

Gopnik, A., Meltzoff, A. and Kuhl, P. (1999) *How Babies Think.* Weidenfeld and Nicolson: London.

Goswami, U. (1998) *Cognition in Children.* Psychology Press: Hove.

Gregg, E. (1968) *What to Do When There is Nothing to Do: A Mother's Handbook – 601 Tested Play Ideas for Young children.* Dell Publishing Co.: New York.

Gura, P. (ed.) directed by Tina Bruce with the Froebel Blockplay Research Group (1992) *Exploring Learning: Young Children and Blockplay.* Paul Chapman Publishing: London.

Gura, P. (1996) *Resources for Early Learning: Children, Adults and Stuff.* Paul Chapman Publishing: London.

Gussin Paley, V. (1984) *Boys and Girls: Superheroes in the Doll Corner.* Chicago University Press: Chicago.

Harris, P. (2000) *The Work of the Imagination.* Blackwell Publishers: Oxford.

Hewitt, P. (2002) Chief Executive, Arts council of England, Extracts from his speech: Beyond Boundaries. *Early Childhood Practice: The Journal for Multi-Professional Practice,* Vol. 4, No. 2, pp. 25–29.

Hofstadter, D. (2000) *Godel, Escher, Bach: An Eternal Golden Braid.* Penguin Books: London.

Holland, P. (2003) *We Don't Play with Guns Here: War, Weapons and Superhero Play in the Early Years.* Open University Press: London and Maidenhead, Philadelphia.

Howkins, J. (2001) *The Creative Economy: How People Make Money from Ideas.* Allen Lane, the Penguin Press: London.

Hutchin, V. (2003) *Observing and Assessing for the Foundation Stage Profile.* Hodder and Stoughton: London.

Hyder, T. (2004) *War, Conflict and Play.* Open University Press: Maidenhead, Philadelphia.

Jansson, T. (2003) *The Summer Book.* Sort of Books, Penguin Group: London.

Karmiloff-Smith, A. (1992) *Beyond Modularity: A Developmental Perspective on Cognitive Science.* A Bradford Book, MIT: Cambridge, MA and London.

Keynes, R. (2002) *Annie's Box.* Fourth Estate: London.

Kitzinger, C. (1997) Born to be good? What motivates us to be good, bad or indifferent towards others? *New Internationalist,* April, pp. 15–17.

Koestler, A. (1975) *The Act of Creation.* Picador, Pan Books Ltd: London.

Laevers, F. (1994) (ed.) *The Innovative Project, 'Experiential Education' and the Definition of Quality in Education.* Katholieke Universiteit: Leuven.

Langer, E. (1997) *The Power of Mindful Learning.* Addison/Wesley Publishing Company: Harlow: England.

Lively, P. (1993) *Cleopatra's Sister.* Penguin Books: Harmondsworth.

Longhorn, F. (1988) *A Sensory Curriculum for Very Special People: A Practical Approach to Curriculum Planning.* Condor Books: Souvenir Press (E and A) Ltd: London.

Mandela, N. (1993) Acceptance Speech of the President of the African National Congress, at the Nobel Peace Prize Award Ceremony, Oslo, Norway. 10th December 1993, www.anc.org.za

Manning-Morton, J. and Thorp, M. (2003) *Key Times for Play.* Open University Press: Maidenhead, Philadelphia.

Marshall, S. (1963) *An Experiment in Education.* Cambridge University Press: Cambridge.

Maslow, A. (1973) *The Farther Reaches of Human Nature.* Penguin: Harmondsworth.

Matterson, E. (1975, 2nd ed) *Play with a Purpose for Under Sevens.* Penguin: Harmondsworth.

Matthews, J. (2003) *Drawing and Painting: Children and Visual Representation.* Paul Chapman Publishing: London.

McKellar, P. (1957) *Imagination and Thinking.* Cohen and West: London.

Murray, L. and Andrews, E. (2000) *The Social Baby.* CP Publishing, Richmond, Surrey.

Nielsen, L. (1992) *Space and Self: Active Learning by Means of the Little Room.* Sikon Press: Copenhagen, Denmark. (Available from RNIB Education.)

Niethammer, C. (1977) *Daughters of the Earth: The Lives and Legends of American Indian Women.* Collier Books, Macmillan Publishing Company: London and NY.

Orr, R. (2003) *My Right to Play: A Child with Complex Needs.* Open University Press: Maidenhead, Philadelphia.

Ouvry, M. (2004) *Sounds Like Play.* Early Education: London.

Papert, S. (1980) *Mind Storms: Children, Computers and Powerful Ideas.* Harvester Press: Brighton.

Piaget, J. (1947) *The Psychology of Intelligence.* Translated by M. Piercy and D. Berlyne. Routledge and Kegan Paul: London.

Piaget, J. (1952) *Play, Dreams and Imitation.* Translated by C. Gattegno and F. Hodgson. Routledge and Kegan Paul: London.

Pound, L. and Harrison, C. (2002) *Supporting Musical Development in the Early Years.* Open University Press: Maidenhead, Philadelphia.

Pullman, P. (2002) A National Curriculum worth having. *Times Educational Supplement, 8th February.*

QCA/DfES (2000) *Curriculum Guidance for the Foundation Stage.* QCA/DfES.

RNIB (1995) *Play it My Way: Learning Through Play with Your Visually Impaired Child.* HMSO, London.

Rowland, P. (1954–55) A three-dimensional face-centred cubic model for the study of crystal phenomena. *Journal of the Institute of Metals*, 1954–55, Vol. 83, pp. 455–495.

Storr, A. (1989) *Solitude.* Harper Collins: London.

Te Whariki (1996) *Early Childhood Curriculum.* New Zealand Ministry of Education. Wellington: Learning Media.

Trevarthen, C. (1998) The child's need to learn a culture, in M. Woodhead, D. Faulkner and K. Littlelton, *Cultural Worlds of Early Childhood.* Routledge in association with Open University Press: London and NY.

Vila, I. (1996) Intentionality, communication and language, in A. Tryphon and J. Voneche, (eds) *Piaget–Vygotsky: The Social Genesis of Thought.* Psychology Press: Hove.

Vygotsky, L. (1978) *Mind in Society.* Harvard University Press: London and Cambridge, MA.

Winnicott, D. (1990) The capacity to be alone. In D. Winnicott, *The Maturational Processes and the Facilitating Environment: Studies in the Theory of Emotional Development.* Karnac Books: London.

Winnicott, D. (1971) *Playing and Reality.* Penguin: Harmondsworth.

Index